TRANSITION TIME

DEDICATION

This book is dedicated to my parents
John and Frances Rosenberg

ACKNOWLEDGMENTS

To all of the parents and grandparents who have
sung these songs and rhymes to their children
through the years and have passed them down,

To all of the children who have played the games
and kept them alive for new generations,

To all of the teachers who so generously shared
their creative ideas with me,

To all of my early childhood students who kept me
on my toes and challenged me to come up with
some new transition "tricks,"

I say, "THANK YOU!"

This book belongs to you!

Jean Feldman

Transition Time

Let's Do Something Different!

By Jean Feldman

Illustrated By Rebecca Jones

Gryphon House

Silver Spring, Maryland

Copyright © 1995 Jean Feldman
Published by Gryphon House, Inc.
10770 Columbia Pike, Suite 201, Silver Spring, MD 20901

Visit us on the web at www.gryphonhouse.com

Cover Design: Graves Fowler Associates
Cover Illustration: Annie Lunsford
Text Illustrations: Rebecca Jones

Reprinted January 2011

Library of Congress Cataloging-in-Publication Data

Feldman , Jean R., 1947–
    Transition time : let's do something different / by Jean Feldman.
        p.   cm.
    Includes index.
    ISBN 978-0-87659-173-4 (pbk.)
    1. Early childhood education-Activity programs. 2. Creative activities and seatwork.   I. Title.
    LB1139.35.A37F47 1995
    372.21—dc20
                                                                95-17456
                                                                CIP

TABLE OF CONTENTS

TABLE OF CONTENTS

Chapter 4—Clean-Up

Chapter 5—Attention Getters

Chapter 6—Line-Up

Chapter 7—Let's Eat and Nap Time

Chapter 11—Stories and Language Activities

Chapter 12—Closure

Children are naturally joyful, active, talkative and energetic. As teachers of young children, one of our most important and challenging roles is to guide them through the many changes in the day. When we prepare children for transitions and focus their attention in positive ways, we eliminate many disruptions. The purpose of this book is to give you insight into how you can make these transitions smooth, meaningful and fun for children. After all, transition activities are really just an indirect way to get children to do what we want them to do without a lot of fuss.

Positive communication is a key. State simply and positively what you want children to do. Instead of "Don't run in the room," try, "Please walk." Rather than, "Sit down and be quiet," say a little finger play that ends with hands in laps. Tell children ahead of time where they are going, what they're going to do and what behavior is expected of them.

It's also important to remember that children can't, don't and won't wait. If you capture their interest with a song, story, prop or poem, then they won't hit, poke or do other things you don't want them to do. Instead, learning skills will be reinforced as you engage them in interesting activities.

Modeling what we want children to do is also a powerful technique for teaching appropriate behavior. Be sure to give them clear examples of what you expect by your own actions, and by pointing out to them children who are responding appropriately.

Above all, children need to be encouraged during transitions. Teachers can be their best coaches, helping them develop self-control as they learn to cooperate and make good choices.

Planning for Transitions

Take a look at your schedule and consider the different transitions:

► as children arrive in the morning

► gathering children for circle time

► cleaning up

► lining up to go outside, to go to lunch, etc.

► settling down for rest

► changing groups or activities

► getting children's attention

► waiting

► ending the day

The above are just a few of the many changes children are expected to make. No wonder they get confused and feel frustrated! Therefore, an important first step is to analyze the day and eliminate as many interruptions as possible.

The planning guide that follows will also be a useful tool. Think about what happens before the transition and what the following activity will be. How can you bridge this with a song, game or learning activity? How much time can you allow for the transition?

What is the purpose of the activity? Children spend a great deal of time changing activities and waiting for the next one to begin. With careful planning, you can capitalize on these "bits of time" with meaningful transitional activities.

If there is a problem, brainstorm to come up with a solution. By anticipating what can go wrong, you can prevent many problems. It will also be helpful to keep some techniques in reserve for emergencies. Write finger plays, songs, games or activity ideas on index cards to keep in your pocket, or wear a pocket apron filled with puppets, toys and other props that will engage children.

Transition Planning Guide	
Transition Time	Activity & materials needed
From To	
From To	
From To	

Schedule

The routine of a daily schedule gives children security and helps them know what to expect, as well as what behavior is expected of them. Rather than keeping to a rigid time frame, consider using time blocks that can be lengthened or shortened depending on the children's interests. Large blocks of time for centers (45 minutes) will

encourage children to become more engaged in activities, play cooperatively, lengthen their attention spans and foster higher level language and thinking skills.

Balance and variety are other important considerations in planning the schedule. Alternate active and quiet periods, as well as large and small group work with independent choices. Provide for integrated learning opportunities which make use of different skills and curriculum areas, and both indoor and outdoor play.

Post a daily schedule for parents as well as children. Take photographs of children involved in different activities to illustrate the different time blocks on the schedule or have children cut pictures from school supply catalogs to illustrate the different time periods.

Our Happy Day		
8:00 - 8:30	🖼	Arrive at School
8:30 - 9:00	🖼	Circle Time
9 - 9:45	🖼	Learning Centers
9:45 - 10:00	🖼	Snack
10:00 - 10:45	🖼	Outdoor Play

Try to give children warnings before changing activities to help them bring closure to their work and prepare for new situations. Also, be sure to plan ample time for transitions so that neither teacher nor children feel rushed.

Developmentally Appropriate Practices

Of utmost importance in planning transitions is choosing activities that are developmentally appropriate for the age, abilities and interests of the children. The activities in this book are suggested for a broad age range and will not be effective with every age group. For example, calendar activities are probably beyond the grasp of two and three year olds, but might be quite meaningful for older children. The younger children might be captivated by your thumb when it becomes a little mouse, while older children might respond more positively to sign language. As their teacher, you know your children better than anyone else and are the best judge of what they will like and what will challenge them. Constantly evaluate transitions by tuning in to children. Observe their reactions and comments, then change and adapt these games and activities to meet their needs.

The philosophy and goals of your program will also influence the activities you select from this book. Some schools allow children to move freely up and down the hall, talking or skipping. Other schools require children to walk in quiet lines. Some classrooms allow children to lounge casually during stories or circle time, while other classes expect children to sit in chairs. Again, you will need to adapt these transitions to the overall expectations for children in your school.

Grouping Strategies

Another effective technique for smooth transitions is to divide the children into small groups. This is sometimes referred to as family grouping strategy or primary care groups. With primary care, the class is divided into two smaller groups, with each teacher responsible for a group of children. Clearly, it is easier to move two small groups of children down the hall or get them settled for nap, rather than trying to handle a large group all at once. Family groupings also enhance bonding, group interactions and language and enable teachers to meet individual needs and be more responsive to the children in their groups. Additionally, parent/teacher communication improves because parents feel closer to one teacher.

Knowing about different transitions and how to plan for them with a variety of activities will make your job easier, your day smoother, your classroom more peaceful and your children happier. Further, when you encourage children to do what you want them to do indirectly with a song or game, they are often more cooperative and, through these positive experiences, develop self-control.

Experiment, change and have fun with the ideas in this book. Think of all the ways you can guide children gently by turning transitions into happy, learning experiences. Be full of surprises! You'll discover how clever you are and that transition time is fun!

DISCIPLINE & TRANSITION TECHNIQUES

Discipline should be viewed as an ongoing process for helping children develop competence, self-control and appropriate behavior. Consider the following principles in guiding children.

1

Know the developmental characteristics for the age that you teach. Many times what teachers think is a discipline problem is actually age-appropriate behavior. Be realistic about expectations and make your program fit children's developmental needs.

2

Children tell us things by their behavior. Become a good observer of children and be sensitive to their needs. If they are wiggly, let them move; if they are frustrated, adapt the activity or change the approach. In addition, work closely with parents to be aware of changes in their home life that could be affecting children's behavior at school.

3

Prevent problems whenever possible. If children continually fight over a toy, get a duplicate. If children are tired and irritable before nap, then change the nap time.

4

Problem-solve and try new techniques. If what you are doing isn't working, then change approaches. Think about what is causing the problem and how you can manipulate the variables to correct it, so children are more successful.

5

Separate children who don't get along. If certain children annoy each other, sit between them at circle time, ask them to play in different areas of the room, etc.

6

Discipline in private. Quietly pull children aside when you need to talk to them. Use "I" messages, rather than "you" messages. Instead of, "You never help pick up," try, "I need your help putting away all the toys." Rather than, "You can't talk to me like that," say, "My feelings get hurt when you talk to me that way." When there is a problem, ask the children what they think they could do to help you solve it.

7

Solve your own problems whenever possible. "Wait until your parents hear about this," or, "I'm sending you to the principal," tells the child that you are not in control and can't handle the situation.

8

Take care of problems immediately. It will have a much more lasting impression on them if the consequence immediately follows the action. Children live in the present and will forget all about an incident if you wait to handle it.

9

Don't expect perfection. Let little things go.

10

Keep a sense of humor. Some of the things children do really are funny and are not major offenses. Don't take yourself or them too seriously, and enjoy a good laugh when things get tense.

11

Empower children by giving them choices and responsibility. "I'm sure you can do it," and other words of encouragement will help them become independent and confident.

12

Use a calm, quiet voice and keep your cool. Whistle a happy tune and pretend you are in control even if you're not.

13

Be consistent. Don't let children do something one day, and then punish them for it the next.

14

Whenever possible, let children work out their own problems. Listen to both sides, then ask them how they would like to handle it. Role-play problem situations, and let children suggest solutions.

15

Use reason to explain rules and implications to children. For example, "It hurts if you hit someone." "We won't have time for a story if you don't clean up now." "You may run when we get outside."

16

Don't end sentences with "Okay?" It sounds like you're doubting yourself or need children's approval. Also, don't ask children if they want to do something if they really don't have a choice. If it's nap time, "Do you want to take a nap?" is really not an option.

17

Be specific with praise and criticism. "Good boy" or "bad girl" means little to children. "I like the way you shared the paints," or "Next time please remember to walk in the hall," are much more effective.

18

Use many positive verbal cues to let children know what behaviors you expect. "Thank you for remembering to wash your hands before lunch." "I like the way Jung pushed in his chair." "Katrina is sitting down and showing me she's ready for our story." These examples all suggest appropriate behaviors for other children to imitate.

19

Use power words like "now" and "it is time." For example, "I want you to sit down now," or "It is time to rest now."

20

Be clear about what is acceptable and unacceptable behavior. Tell children what you expect ahead of time and be clear about what is not appropriate behavior.

21

Set up the room in learning centers so children can be successful and work in smaller groups.

22

Give children lots of opportunities to move and vent their energy. Let them wiggle, exercise, run outside, etc. Tell them they can squeeze play dough, kick a ball (outside) or hit a pillow when they are angry. Also, take some old socks and tie knots in them. When children are frustrated, let them pull the knots out of the socks.

23

Respect children's differences. Accept their different values, backgrounds and cultures as well as their unique ways of solving problems.

24

Give children unconditional love and support. Don't withdraw your love or base your attention on how they behave.

25

Be patient. It takes a long time for children to grow up. They need to be gently guided, rather than pushed or rushed.

Everyone loses if you

▶ Yell or use physical punishment

▶ Argue or get in a power struggle

▶ Bribe children or make empty threats

▶ Embarrass children in front of the class

▶ Use food to control children

Everyone wins if you

▶ Distract children—get their attention with a different toy, activity, song or game. When a child is upset, try to engage her in a favorite activity. If children are fighting over a toy, offer one a different toy.

▶ Redirect children—give them a similar activity that is more appropriate. If a child can't keep her hands to herself at circle, give her a sponge ball or a small toy to hold. If a child runs in the room, tell him he can run outside, but he needs to use walking feet inside.

▶ Tell children to use words—words empower children to handle their own problems and allow them to release feelings in acceptable ways.

▶ Help children deal with the natural consequences of their behavior —accepting natural consequences will help children make the connection between how they behave and its effect on others. If they knock someone's tower of blocks over, they should help her build it again; if they spill the paints, they should clean them up; if they make someone cry, they should comfort that person and try to make him feel better.

▶ Give children choices—offer children two choices, the results of which will lead to a desired outcome. Choices allow both children and teachers to win, and the child feels like she has some control. For example, "Do you want to lie down with your head at this end or that end of your cot for nap?" "Would you like to share the red car or the blue car with Tasha?"

▶ Use nonverbal language—look at children when you want them to stop doing something, walk over to them or use other facial and body expressions to convey what you want them to do.

▶ Take advantage of "teachable" times by showing children appropriate ways to behave.

 DISTRACTION

Waiting List

When?

Try a waiting list for a popular center, toy or other activity indoors or out on the playground.

Why?

Children learn how useful writing can be, and they learn to take turns.

What?

clipboard
paper
pen or pencil

How?

▶ Hang the waiting list near the art easel, outside by the riding toys or next to any crowded center in the room.

▶ Explain to the children the number limit for each center and discuss why they have to wait or take turns.

▶ To help everyone remember whose turn is next, tell them to look at the waiting list.

▶ If they want to play there, they can ask the teacher to write their names on the list.

▶ When someone leaves, she should scratch her name or mark off the top of the list so you will know who gets the next turn.

Adaptations

▶ Make a list for children to sign up for show and tell or other activities.

▶ Encourage children who can't write their names to make special marks or draw small pictures to identify themselves.

▶▶▶▶▶▶▶   DISTRACTION   ▶▶▶▶▶▶▶

Official Class Report

When?

The next time a child starts to complain or tattle, try using this technique.

Why?

The Official Report not only gives children an opportunity to vent their thoughts and feelings, but also shows how useful writing can be.

What?

notebook with Official Class Report
   printed on it
pencil or pen

How?

▶ Tell the children about the Official Class Report.

▶ It is a place to record their concerns.

▶ Discuss the difference between major emergencies and less serious situations.

▶ When a child comes to whine or tell on someone, give her the notebook. Ask her to draw a picture about what happened.

▶ Ask her to dictate the story of what happened. Write the child's account in the book.

Adaptation

▶ Make a teacher's mailbox (from a shoe box or detergent box) for children to leave special messages. These could be pictures the children draw to express complaints, ideas, secrets or personal matters.

 DISTRACTION

Boo Boo Bunny

When?

Use Boo Boo Bunny when children get little hurts or bumps.

Why?

The bunny distracts children and the ice helps their hurt.

What?

washcloth
thin ribbon
pompom
wiggly eyes
glue
plastic ice cube

Preparation

► Fold the washcloth in half diagonally to make a triangle.

► Starting at the top point, roll up tightly.

► Fold in half; tie off the head with the ribbon and bend back the pointed ends to make ears.

► Glue on eyes and a pompom tail.

How?

► Freeze the plastic ice cube.

► When a child is hurt, get Boo Boo Bunny to make them feel better.

► Insert the ice cube in the bunny's body and let the child apply it to their hurt.

Adaptation

► If one child has hurt another child, then let the child responsible for the accident get Boo Boo Bunny to help comfort the hurt child. This helps children learn to be responsible for their behavior.

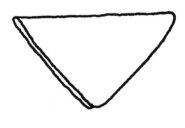

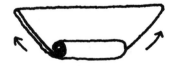

▶▶▶▶▶▶ DISTRACTION ▶▶▶▶▶▶

Magic Water

When?

When a child is hurt or upset, this distraction helps to calm him down.

Why?

Focusing on the water helps children regain their self-composure. They might also believe in its benefits!

What?

paper cup
drinking water
special pitcher (optional)

How?

▶ If a child has a little tumble or if he is frustrated or upset, hold him and give him some Magic Water.

▶ Fill a cup with water and hand it to him.

▶ After he drinks it, ask him if he feels better and wants to talk about it.

Adaptation

▶ Keep a small, special pitcher on your desk, perhaps a beautiful pottery one, to hold the Magic Water. This is much more special than pouring water from the tap!

 DISTRACTION

Behavior Log

When?

If a child is having difficulty adjusting in class, carefully observe the child and keep a written account of different instances when this occurs.

Why?

Children's behavior tells us things, so by recording it, patterns or causes for the behavior may become clear.

What?

notebook and pen or pencil

How?

▶ Record incidents of misbehavior or disruptions as soon as possible after they happen.

▶ Write down what went on before the incident or what might have triggered it. Watch, observe and try to figure out what's going on to cause a child to behave in such a way.

▶ Think about how to modify the program so the child will be more successful.

▶ Communicate findings with parents and school administrators.

 DISTRACTION ▶▶▶▶▶▶

The Book

When?

If a young child questions the rules or why she has to do something, The Book is the perfect solution.

Why?

Some children challenge rules. This technique helps them see that we all have guidelines that we must follow. It further illustrates how words and writing are useful and functional.

What?

The Book (copy of state regulations, licensing criteria and/or school policies)

How?

▶ Place The Book in an obvious place in the room.

▶ When a child asks questions about certain aspects of the program, for example, why she has to take a nap or why she can't fight, pull the book off the shelf and firmly tell her, "because The Book says so."

▶ Find the section in the book relating to naps or the rules in question and read it to the child.

▶ Talk about why she thinks that rule exists.

▶ Most children will be quite satisfied knowing that you didn't just make up nap time or other rules, and that even teachers have guidelines which they must follow.

Adaptation

▶ Make a class rule book by letting children draw pictures and dictate sentences about different rules.

 **DISTRACTION** ▶▶▶▶▶▶▶

Do the Walk

When?

If a child loses control and is disturbing the class, taking a walk may help him regain composure without upsetting the rest of the children.

Why?

Some children do not know how to cope with frustration or anger in acceptable ways. A walk and change of scenery may help them vent those feelings.

What?

No materials are needed.

How?

▶ When a child becomes disruptive and loses control, firmly take him by the hand and say, "We're going for a walk outside."

▶ Let the other teacher take over.

▶ Leave the room and walk outside or in a quiet area of the building.

▶ Remain calm and let him scream; just keep on walking.

▶ It may also help to let him run around on the playground or in the gym.

▶ Or let him squeeze play dough, hit a punching bag or do some other physical activity.

▶ When he's spent his energy and seems more calm ask, "Are you ready to go back to the room now?"

▶ This is often an effective alternative for children when they become overwhelmed.

Adaptation

▶ Call a school administrator to take the child for a walk or run out on the playground if there is only one teacher in the room.

Carrots to Bite

When?

Biters? Fortunately, biting is just a phase some children go through. This technique offers some relief until they outgrow it.

Why?

Children bite because they don't have the language or other skills to communicate their feelings, or because their gums are sore. Chewy carrots make their gums feel better and distract them from biting.

What?

raw carrots, celery, apple slices or other crunchy food
baggie

How?

➤ Give the child a bag of carrot sticks to carry in her pockets or keep in her cubby.

➤ Tell her that when she is angry to use her words, then bite a carrot to make her feel better.

Adaptation

➤ Encourage children who bite to get ice, a cold rag or a stuffed toy to help comfort the child they have hurt.

▶▶▶▶▶▶ CHOICES ▶▶▶▶▶▶

Voting

When?

Children enjoy voting for games they want to play, which story they want you to read and other activities.

Why?

When children are given choices, they feel empowered and are more likely to cooperate. They begin to understand the process of majority rule and that sometimes they get their way, and sometimes they don't.

What?

No materials are needed.

How?

- ▶ Give children two options for a game to play or a story you will read.
- ▶ Tell each child to raise his hand or stand up when he hears the one he wants.
- ▶ Carefully count aloud the children voting for each option.
- ▶ Then ask, "Which is more?"
- ▶ Follow through on the children's requests.

Adaptations

- ▶ Tally responses on the board, or use a graph to show comparisons.
- ▶ Let children vote on snacks, room themes, field trips and other decisions.

 RELEASING ENERGY

Let's Go Skating

When?

When the weather outside is frightful, have some fun inside.

Why?

Wiggles and energy will skate away.

What?

inexpensive paper plates (two for
  each child)
tape or record

How?

► This activity is safe to play on the rug. It should not be attempted on a bare floor or linoleum surface.

► Give each child two paper plates.

► Have them put the plates on the floor and stand on them.

► Ask them to see if they can skate around the room by sliding their feet.

► Remind them to be careful not to bump into anyone.

► Play music and let them skate around the room.

► Challenge them to skate backwards, balance on one foot, jump up and turn around on the plates, etc.

Adaptation

► Vary the style and tempo of the skating music.

 RELEASING ENERGY

Rag Doll and Soldier

When?

If children are tense, relieve stress by pretending to be rag dolls and soldiers.

Why?

Tightening and relaxing muscles is an effective way to relax.

What?

No materials are needed.

How?

- ➤ Ask the children to stand up.
- ➤ Demonstrate the motions for the children.
- ➤ Ask them to follow along.
- ➤ Stand up straight and tall like a soldier. Be very stiff. Don't move. Hold it.
- ➤ Now, bend over and be floppy like a rag doll. Let arms dangle.

- ➤ Relax all over.
- ➤ Be a soldier again, straight and tall.
- ➤ Be a rag doll, loose and floppy.
- ➤ Soldier!
- ➤ Rag doll!
- ➤ Continue calling out "Soldier" and "Rag doll" as the children tighten, then let go.

Adaptations

- ➤ Have the children pretend to be jelly-fish and shake all over.
- ➤ Then ask them to shake various parts of the body such as their arms, legs, heads, backs, etc.
- ➤ Help children relax by doing breathing exercises. Have them breathe deep, fast, slow, etc.
- ➤ Use this activity at nap time to relax children.

 RELEASING ENERGY

Back Rub a Dub

When?

Calm children with this group activity after an active period or when they are all "wound up."

Why?

Children learn to relax as they are kind to each other.

What?

No materials are needed.

How?

➤ Have the children stand in a line with their hands on the shoulders of the person in front of them.

➤ Demonstrate the following exercise.

➤ Massage the shoulders of the person in front of you.

➤ Softly scratch the person's back.

➤ Do gentle chops with the sides of your hands.

➤ Make raindrops pitter patter on the person's back with your fingertips.

➤ Turn and face the opposite direction.

➤ Put your hands on the shoulders of the person who is now in front of you and return the back rub as above.

Adaptation

➤ Teach children how to give a self-massage. Have them stretch out their legs and rub them slowly up and down like trains going back and forth (fast, then slow). Next, rub arms up and down like an elevator (fast, then slow). Massage other body parts such as face, head or feet. Massage hands with lotion.

 RELEASING ENERGY

Exercise Bike

When?

Many times when children are out of control, they just need a little exercise break.

Why?

Exercise is a positive way to release energy and vent frustrations.

What?

No materials are needed.

How?

➤ Ask the children to lie down on their backs, put their legs in the air and pretend that they are riding a bike.

➤ Tell them to pedal slowly since they are riding in the country.

➤ Pretend to pass various animals and sites. Ask them what they see as they are riding their bikes.

➤ Pretend to ride up a steep hill, then race down the other side.

➤ When all the wiggles are out, have the children put down their legs, breathe deeply, close their eyes and relax.

Adaptations

➤ Have children stand up and pretend to climb a ladder, reaching with alternating arms as they lift their legs. Challenge them to count how many rungs they can climb. When they can't climb any further, tell them to sit down and relax.

➤ Ask children to sit on the floor, choose a partner, extend their legs so their feet touch their partner's, and hold hands with their partner. Tell them to pretend that they are rowing a boat as they rock back and forth. Sing "Row, Row, Row Your Boat."

 RELEASING ENERGY

Dancing Hands Picture

When?

This creative project is fun on a rainy day or when children are full of wiggles.

Why?

Feelings and frustrations are released as children dance their crayons over the paper.

What?

butcher paper
crayons
tape or record

How?

▶ Roll out a long sheet of butcher paper on the floor.

▶ Give each child two crayons—one for each hand.

▶ Ask them to lie down on their backs in a line on the floor with their hands above their heads, touching the butcher paper.

▶ When the music starts, tell them to begin drawing with the crayons on the paper.

Adaptations

▶ Cover a table with a large sheet of paper. Give the children a crayon for each hand and have them stand around the table. Let their crayons dance on the paper as they listen to music.

▶ Put some contact paper on the floor with the sticky side up. Tape down the ends, then let the children take off their shoes and dance or tiptoe on the sticky paper.

 RELEASING ENERGY

Paper Balls

When?

Use paper balls to release wiggles or when children need a change of pace.

Why?

Throwing paper balls is a positive way to get rid of energy or frustration.

What?

scrap paper

How?

- ▶ Give each child a piece of scrap paper.

- ▶ Ask them to wad it up into a ball.

- ▶ Divide the group into two teams and have them face each other about 10-20 feet apart.

- ▶ On the word "go," both teams throw their balls at each other.

- ▶ If a ball lands on the other side, that side quickly picks it up and throws it back at the other team.

- ▶ When "freeze" is called, they must stop throwing and gather up the balls on their side.

- ▶ Each team counts their balls, and the team with the least number wins.

Adaptations

- ▶ Play several rounds of the game and tally scores at the end.

- ▶ Let the children play this game on the playground.

GOOD MORNING!

How you start the morning can influence the mood for the rest of the day. A smile, a positive attitude and enthusiasm for the activities will certainly be a catalyst for the children in your room.

Prepare materials and learning centers before the children arrive. Then you will be free to focus your attention on the children, and you will have time to communicate with them and their parents. Place inviting materials such as puzzles, play dough, collage materials, books and games out on the tables and in the learning centers to get children actively engaged. Offer a wide variety of toys and experiences from which the children may choose. Rotate materials and continually add new props and interesting objects to centers. Give children something exciting to look forward to each day when they come to school!

Children love to hear their names. They enjoy seeing you and hearing a cheerful hello every morning. Individual greetings such as "I'm glad to see you, Sarah," "Good morning, Kimo," and "We're going to have a great day, Kendra," will let each child know how important he or she is. Position yourself near the door. Bend down to the child's eye level to speak to her. A gentle touch, hug or smile also reassures children. Sometimes it's fun to surprise children in the morning with a hat, puppet, stuffed animal or other prop that will create interest for an activity that you have planned that day.

Easing Separations

Saying good-bye to parents can be a difficult transition for little ones. It is particularly important for adults to be sensitive to children's feelings and to help ease the stress. If possible, visit the home before school starts and find out as much as you can about the child, her likes and dislikes and the home environment. You may want to prepare a "Welcome Book" for the child with a list of the other children in the room, a photocopied picture of the school and teachers, a list of favorite activities, the daily schedule, a story about exciting things they will do during the year, etc. Talk to the parents and help them feel comfortable; let them know that they can get involved in the school. An open house, pot luck dinner or other social event for families before school begins makes them feel more at ease. It is also helpful to invite small groups of children for a "tea party" before the first day or to stagger starting dates so that the entire class won't start all together. This gives you and the new children a little extra time to get used to one another and the classroom.

Ask children to bring a family photo to school as well as a favorite toy or object from home. A cubby with the child's name will give him or her a sense of belonging and a special place to put his or her things. Children have different styles. Some will jump right in, while others will need more time and support. Be available to sing to them, rock them, read them a story or distract them with a favorite toy or an activity to do with a special friend. Bridge the gap between home and school by letting the child draw a picture to take home or use a play phone to call home. Help children verbalize their feelings and frustrations, and be patient and supportive until they feel secure and settle in.

Encourage parents to spend some time in the classroom each day before leaving their child. They might want to read a story, work a puzzle or do a collage together. Tell parents they should always say good-bye to their children when it's time to leave. Rituals such as a kiss, hug and reassuring word about how much they love them and when they'll return to pick them up, can mean a great deal to children. Discourage parents from leaving without saying good-bye or lingering or coming back once they have said good-bye.

Hang a poster (similar to the one shown) on the back of your door as a friendly reminder to parents before they leave their child.

Did you remember to . . .

Kiss me?

Hug me?

Say good-bye to me?

Tell me you'll be back?

 WELCOME

Happy Boxes

When?

Offer children who arrive early or stay late something special to capture their attention and keep them interested.

Why?

Happy boxes reinforce learning skills, encourage creativity and improve children's attention span.

What?

large detergent boxes with plastic handles (Ask parents to save them for you.)
spray paint
toys, collections, art supplies, etc. (See list on following page.)

Preparation

- ▶ Remove the plastic handle from the detergent box.

- ▶ Spray paint the box, dry, then put the handle back on.

- ▶ Fill with fun, challenging materials that will interest children.

How?

- ▶ Place the happy boxes on the floor or tables before the children arrive.

- ▶ Children play with the contents of the boxes individually or with a friend.

- ▶ Encourage the children to put the materials away before taking another box.

Adaptations

- ▶ Cover the boxes with contact paper, wallpaper, fabric, collage materials or let the children decorate them.

- ▶ Rotate the materials in the boxes weekly, or keep making new happy boxes to add to your collection.

- ▶ Let children take the boxes home with them. (This is a good way to get parents involved, while giving them ideas for materials for their children.)

- ▶ Have children play with the materials from happy boxes on a carpet square or inside a hula hoop.

- ▶ Give the boxes to children who wake up early from naps so they have something quiet to do.

Happy Box Ideas

Here are suggestions for materials to put in Happy Boxes. These self-contained activities can entertain one or more children, or enhance the learning centers in the classroom. They're inexpensive, versatile and fun!

- blank books, pencils, pens, crayons
- play dough, small rolling pin, cookie cutters
- plastic or wooden animals or characters
- toy cars, trucks, road signs
- hole punch and paper
- puppets
- flannel board stories and small felt board
- birthday party paper products (hats, plates, cups, etc.)
- plastic dinosaurs
- squeeze toys
- buttons, spools, pasta with holes and other materials that can be strung
- junk mail
- paper, crayons, markers
- sticky notes, envelopes, pens and writing paraphernalia
- grab bag art—fill with odds and ends
- musical instruments
- magnets, magnifying glasses
- pegboard, pegs and pattern pictures
- books
- bandaids, stethoscope
- picture box (photographs of friends and families)
- plastic food
- timer and stop watch
- nature collections (leaves, nuts, shells, rocks, etc.)
- sewing cards
- flashlight
- play money
- puzzles
- old jewelry
- different textures to feel
- deck of cards
- things to smell
- letter boxes (collect things beginning with a certain sound)
- color boxes (collect objects of a certain color)
- baby doll, clothes, blanket
- objects to sort (buttons, money, assorted rocks, etc.)
- story boxes (characters for acting out a story such as "The Three Bears" or "The Little Red Hen")
- action characters
- tape measure, ruler
- restaurant menu, pad, pencil, paper products
- theme boxes (circus, underwater, community helpers, etc.)
- plastic interlocking blocks
- concentration cards or games

 WELCOME

Pools of Fun

When?

A swimming pool gives children something to "dive" into when they come to school.

Why?

Children play with materials in a defined space which helps them focus their attention as they arrive.

What?

plastic swimming pool (empty)

Preparation

Fill the pool with one of the following materials.
- books and pillows
- paper, pencils, markers
- blocks
- plastic or wooden animals (zoo, farm)
- math counters
- small cars and trucks
- musical instruments
- clay or play dough
- natural objects (rocks, shells, leaves, etc.)

- manipulatives (stringing beads, stacking toys, pegboard, etc.)
- puzzles
- dolls, blankets, clothes
- paper, hole punch, scissors
- sewing cards
- puppets
- art supplies
- card games
- sensory materials
- magnets or color paddles

How?

▶ Place the pool in a quiet corner.

▶ Tell the children there will be something fun in there for them every day.

▶ Limit the number of children who can play in the pool to one or two at a time.

▶ Remind them about cleaning up when they get ready to leave.

Adaptations

▶ Use several pools in different areas of the room.

▶ Have a "Turns" list so children can sign up for a turn to play in the pool.

Look Who's Here Today!

When?

Children look forward to signing in each day when they arrive at school.

Why?

In addition to learning that it's important for them to come to school and that they are missed when they are absent, a sign-in chart encourages children to recognize their names and accept responsibility.

What?

colored construction paper
scissors
markers
hole punch
yarn
tape
push pins or stick-on tabs with hooks
basket or shallow box
bulletin board or poster board

Preparation

▶ Cut balloon shapes out of construction paper.

▶ Write a child's name on each balloon. Punch a hole at the top, then tape a 3" piece of yarn to the bottom of each balloon.

▶ Let the children hang up their balloons. Use push pins with a bulletin board, or stick-on tabs with hooks with poster board.

How?

▶ Place the children's name balloons in a basket.

▶ As they arrive in the morning, help them find their names and hang them on the board.

▶ At first you will need to help the children with this, but they will quickly learn how to do it by themselves.

Adaptations

▶ Change name tags for seasons or monthly themes. Use apples, pumpkins, ornaments, hearts, kites, flowers, fish, etc.

▶ Envelopes or library pockets can be used in place of hooks. Make tall objects, like paper dolls or crayons, that the each child can place in the envelope that has his name on it.

Feeling Faces

When?

Use Feeling Faces to help children express their mood.

Why?

It is important to accept children's feelings and recognize their emotional state. This activity encourages children to talk about how they're feeling inside.

What?

envelopes or library pockets
poster board
tagboard or heavy paper
markers
scissors
glue

Preparation

▶ Use library pockets or cut the envelopes in half to form small pockets. Print each child's name on a pocket and glue it to the poster board.

▶ Cut the tagboard into 2-1/2" x 6" rectangles that will fit into the pockets.

▶ Draw one of the four expressions illustrated on the bottom ends of each side of the card.

How?

▶ Place the feeling cards in a basket near the name envelopes.

▶ As the children come in the room, let them select a card and place it in their name envelopes to show the face which most closely resembles how they feel.

▶ Be available to listen to them if they want to talk about their feelings.

Adaptations

▶ Let children draw their own expressions on blank cards.

▶ Encourage the children to change the faces in their pockets during the day as their feelings change.

 WHO'S HERE?

Helping Hands

When?

Children check the job chart each morning to see what their responsibilities will be.

Why?

Classroom jobs help children feel important, develop respect for school materials and encourage children to be responsible.

What?

heavy poster board or plywood (3' x 3')
hooks
construction paper or tagboard
markers
scissors
hole punch
glue

Preparation

► Think of a list of jobs for the classroom. Try to have enough so that each child can have a job. Here are a few suggestions.

- line leader
- caboose
- librarian
- table monitors (3 or 4)
- housekeeper (home living area)
- water plants
- feed pets
- messenger (run errands)
- outdoor toys
- sweeper
- door holder
- art director (clean art area)
- calendar helper
- song leader
- weather person
- trash collector
- flag leader
- chairs (push in)
- riders (first on riding toys)

▶ Write the jobs on the poster board or plywood and draw or glue on a picture clue for each. Attach a hook by each job.

▶ Cut the construction paper or tagboard in 1-1/2" x 2-1/2" rectangles. Print the children's names on these cards and punch a hole in the top of each one.

▶ Hang a child's name by each job.

How?

▶ Discuss the various jobs in the classroom.

▶ Give clear directions about what each of the responsibilities involve.

▶ Carefully teach the children how to do each job, or let the children train each other.

▶ As they come in each day, the children find their names and check what their jobs will be.

▶ Praise children when they remember their jobs, and prompt those who forget.

▶ Rotate the jobs weekly so all children get to experience different tasks.

▶ Add or delete jobs as needed.

Adaptations

▶ Let each child choose what they would like to do by hanging her name by a job when she comes in.

▶ Use the job board as a sign-in board as well. Make two name cards for every child from two different colors of construction paper such as red and yellow. Before the children come to school, hang the red name tags by assigned jobs. Upon arrival, each child finds her yellow name tag and hangs it on top of the red one. This way it is also easy to see who is absent.

▶ Use library pockets on a bulletin board for classroom jobs. "Busy Bees" and "Super Stars" are titles that could be used for the job board.

 **WHO'S HERE?**

Kings, Queens and Helpers

When?

This idea gives different children turns to be line leader and classroom helper each day.

Why?

In addition to building responsibility and contributing to their self-esteem, children learn how to wait for a turn.

What?

cardboard
aluminum foil
scissors
glue
glitter or sequins
large paper clips

Preparation

▶ Cut out two cardboard crowns approximately 22" x 3" similar to the illustration.

▶ Cover the crowns with aluminum foil and decorate with glitter or sequins.

▶ Adjust the crown to the child's head, then secure in place with a paper clip.

How?

▶ Using the list of children in the class, choose one child each day to be the king or queen.

▶ The next child on the list is the king's or queen's helper for the day.

▶ The king or queen gets to wear the crown, be the line leader and run errands for the teacher.

▶ The royal helper also wears a crown, stands at the end of the line and is responsible for closing the door. (They are usually happy to do this as they can anticipate being the king or queen the following day.)

▶ Continue down the list until each child has had a turn to be the king or queen and the helper, then begin the list again.

Adaptation

▶ Use hats, aprons or buttons to designate the line leader, caboose or other special helpers.

 WHO'S HERE?

Helper Can

When?

The helper assists the teacher with errands or special jobs.

Why?

Children appreciate the fairness of this idea and enjoy helping the teacher.

What?

coffee can
2" squares of paper
markers
scissors
glue
wrapping paper, wallpaper, contact paper or spray paint
envelope

Preparation

▶ Decorate the can with paper or spray paint.

▶ Print each child's name on a 2" square, then put all the names in the can.

How?

▶ When there is a special job to be done, pull a child's name out of the can.

▶ After this child has had a turn, put her name in the envelope.

▶ When every child has been a helper, remove the names from the envelope, put them in the can and begin all over again.

Adaptation

▶ Pull out children's names to choose a song or book, or to choose a child to sit by you at circle time or have another special favor.

Cozy Corner

When?

Some children like a little private time when they arrive in the morning, while other children need to be alone at other times during the day.

Why?

There is very little privacy for children in most school environments, so it's important to have a place where they can get away from the group and be alone.

What?

appliance box or other large box
sharp knife
markers or paints
pillows, soft animals and books

Preparation

▶ Cut a door and windows in the box with a sharp knife. (An adult will need to do this.)

▶ Let the children decorate the box with paints or markers.

▶ Place the box in a quiet area of the room and fill with pillows, soft animals and books.

How?

▶ Discuss different feelings with the children and tell them that you understand that sometimes they want to be with other people, but sometimes they just want to be by themselves.

▶ Tell the children that when they want to be alone they can go to the Cozy Corner to think, read a book, dream or relax. (Limit the number of children who can use this space at the same time to one or two.)

Adaptations

▶ Use old blankets, sheets or scarves to create a "dream center."

▶ Hang stars inside and fill with pillows or large beanbags.

▶ Create a private space by pulling a bookshelf away from a wall, or filling a large plastic cube with pillows and blankets.

▶ Add a listening center with some peaceful music or environmental sounds to the Cozy Corner.

▶▶▶▶▶▶▶ 3 ▶▶▶▶▶▶▶

CIRCLE TIME

Many early childhood teachers start their day in a special way with circle time. It is a time for creating a feeling of community and togetherness, and a ritual that children look forward to. The length of time spent in a large group activity such as this varies according to the age and attention span of the children. The secret of a good circle time is to keep it short and interesting with a variety of activities and materials. Generally, children should not be forced to participate in circle time, but if you have something fun for them to see or do, they won't want to miss out.

If there are two teachers, another suggestion for circle time is to break the large group into two smaller groups to enable more participation and individualization.

A comfortable way to initiate circle time is to sit casually on the floor with the children and begin singing a song. Sit cross-legged and the children will do the same. Encourage them to "sit like a pretzel" or "crisscross applesauce." Some teachers prefer to sit in chairs. Some use carpet squares or a special blanket to define the space for their group, while in other classrooms children just lounge casually on their tummies, backs or sides.

Informal conversations, songs, stories, finger plays and poems enhance feelings of fellowship at circle time. This group meeting is a perfect time to make plans, explain new activities and materials and involve children in making decisions about what they want to do each day. New concepts, themes and other information can also be introduced at circle time. Capture children's attention and start the day with good feelings by using the tunes, rhymes and props in this chapter.

Make-Believe Microphone

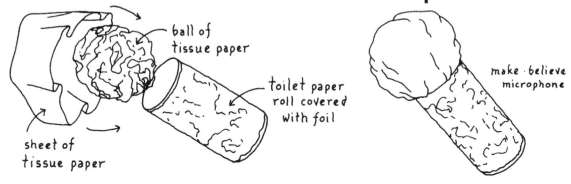

ball of tissue paper

toilet paper roll covered with foil

sheet of tissue paper

make-believe microphone

When?

A make-believe microphone is a unique way to start circle time or get children to listen.

Why?

In addition to giving children a chance to perform, the microphone encourages language development.

What?

cardboard roll (from toilet paper or paper towels)
aluminum foil
black tissue paper
glue

Preparation

▶ Cover the cardboard roll with aluminum foil.

▶ Cut the sheet of tissue paper in half. Wad up one half to form a ball, then cover it with the other half.

▶ Twist the loose ends of the tissue paper into the cardboard roll and glue it in place.

How?

▶ When the children are sitting quietly for circle time, pretend to speak into the microphone. Give directions or sing a song.

▶ Pass the microphone around and let each child say good morning, sing his name or tell what he's looking forward to doing that day.

▶ Never force children to say something into the microphone. When they feel comfortable and secure in the group, they will generally be willing to share.

Adaptations

▶ Children can use the microphone to lead the class in a song, say a joke or tell a story.

▶ Let the children take turns talking into a tape recorder, then play it back and see if they can identify their voices.

▶▶▶▶▶▶ CHILDREN'S PROPS ▶▶▶▶▶▶

Talking Stick

When?

Use the talking stick during circle time, large group activities and class discussions.

Why?

Children learn how to take turns and listen when others are talking by using this stick.

What?

stick or dowel (12" long)
gold or silver spray paint
glue
glitter or sequins

Preparation

▶ Spray the stick with the paint and let it dry.

▶ Decorate with glitter and sequins.

How?

▶ Show the children the talking stick and explain that only the person holding the stick can talk. Everyone else must listen until it's their turn to hold the stick.

▶ Begin passing the stick around the circle and listening attentively.

▶ Let the children say whatever they want, or focus the discussion with a topic or question.

▶ The teacher brings closure to the discussion when the stick returns to him or her.

Adaptations

▶ Pass the talking stick around when telling circle stories.

▶ Let children choose to whom they would like to pass the stick.

▶ To make a simple talking stick, simply cover a pencil with aluminum foil or wrapping paper.

▶ Use the talking stick at the end of the day for children to recall what they have done at school.

Tickets

When?

Try this idea to entice children to come to circle time or a story.

Why?

These tickets make children feel like they're going to do something special, and motivate them to be a part of the group.

What?

colored paper
scissors
can with a plastic lid
tape

Preparation

► Using the illustration or your own ideas, make tickets from colored paper.

► Decorate the can and cut a slit in the lid.

How?

► As the children arrive in the morning, hand each one a ticket.

► Tell them to hold on to them so they can come to a special circle time.

► Encourage the children to put the ticket in their pockets. Tape the tickets to them if they have no pockets.

► Or, give the tickets to the children as they clean up.

► Let the children put their tickets into the slot in the can lid as they join the group.

Adaptations

► Choose a child to help collect the tickets.

► Make tickets for various centers in the room or for outdoor activities. It might be just what is needed to involve children in new activities.

Magic Blanket

When?

A magic blanket is the perfect way to get little ones to settle down for a story or group activity.

Why?

The blanket gives children a defined space and a place to sit.

What?

blanket, quilt, bedspread or parachute

How?

▶ Shake the blanket in the air and say, "It's magic blanket time. Come and join me on the magic blanket."

▶ Sit down and model appropriate circle time behavior.

▶ Welcome the children with a smile or by using their names.

▶ When most of the children are in the circle, sing a song or begin a finger play.

Adaptations

▶ Take the magic blanket outdoors and use it for a story or a sing-a-long on the playground.

▶ Lay on the blanket outdoors and look for pictures in the clouds.

▶ Have children put their legs under the blanket and hold the edge with their hands. (Keeps busy feet and hands out of trouble!)

▶ Include children in making their own magic blanket by having them color an old sheet with markers or fabric crayons.

▶ Make individual felt mats for the children to sit on at circle time. Purchase felt squares and decorate them with the children's names. Place the name mats randomly in a circle, then help the children find their names and sit down.

New Shoes Dance

 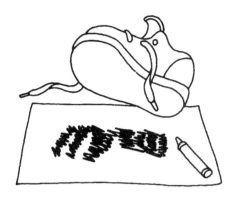 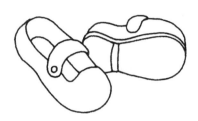

When?

How special it is when youngsters get a new pair of shoes! This song will add to their joy.

Why?

This song gives children individual attention and enhances their self-esteem.

What?

No materials are needed.

How?

► When a child wears new shoes to school, invite him to stand in the middle of the group.

► Sing the following song to the tune of "This Old Man."

Here's one foot. (stick out one foot)
Here are two. (hold out other foot)
Each is wearing a brand new shoe.
So skip and dance all around the floor. (child dances or skips around the circle)
That's what these new shoes are for!

Adaptations

► Do a graph of the different kinds of shoes the children wear.

► Let children do sole rubbings of the bottoms of each other's shoes. Use paper and a crayon with the paper peeled off. Place the paper over the bottom of a shoe or sneaker and rub with the flat side of the crayon until the design appears.

► Bring in different sizes and styles of shoes and other footwear, for example, baby shoes, slippers, work boots, sandals, high heels, athletic shoes, ballet shoes, etc. Discuss who would wear the shoes and why, then let the children play with them in the housekeeping area.

► Have each child take off one shoe and place it in a pile in the middle of the floor. Tell the children to close their eyes as you take the shoes and hide them around the room in plain sight. Then let them go and hunt for their shoes. They can sit down and put them back on when they find them.

 **SONGS & RHYMES**

This Little Girl

When?

Help children calm down for circle time with this finger play, or use it to relax them at rest time.

Why?

Finger plays keep little hands busy and develop auditory memory and language skills.

What?

No materials are needed.

How?

▶ Hold up the right index finger and say, "This little girl is ready to start her day, are you? Show me by holding your finger in the air."

▶ When the children have their fingers in the air, begin the following poem.

This little girl is ready for bed, (wiggle finger)
On the pillow she lays her head. (lay finger in palm)
Wrap the covers around her tight. (fold fingers around)
That's the way she spends the night. (rock finger)
Morning comes she opens her eyes.
Off with a toss the covers fly. (uncurl fingers)

She puts on her clothes, (pretend to dress finger and feed)
Eats her breakfast,
Brushes her teeth, (brush teeth)
And combs her hair. (comb hair)
Now she's ready and on her way,
To work and play at school
All day.

This little boy... (do the poem with the other index finger, pretending it is a little boy)

Adaptations

▶ Draw little faces with felt tip markers on your index finger.

▶ Try this finger play to focus children's attention.

Two little houses shut up tight. (hold fists up)
Open the doors and let in the light. (open fingers)
Ten little finger people (hold up fingers)
Tall and straight
Ready for school
At half past eight.

▶ Change the words to fit the group, for example,

Ten little finger people
Standing in line
Ready for kindergarten
Right at nine.

 SONGS & RHYMES

I'm So Glad I Came to School

When?

Start circle time with a smile and this song.

Why?

Children will learn the name of their school and develop a sense of belonging to the school group.

What?

bell

How?

▶ Ring a little bell, then begin this chant.

I'm so glad I came to school today,
I came to school today,
I came to school today,
I'm so glad I came to school today,
I came to be with all my friends.
I'm so glad I came to (name school) today,
I came to (name school) today,
I came to (name school) today,
I'm so glad I came to (name school) today,
I came to be with all my friends.

▶ Ask the children why they're happy to be at school and what they're looking forward to doing that day.

Adaptation

▶ Here's a song to build school identity. Sing it to the tune of "Here We Go 'Round the Mulberry Bush."

The name of my school is (name school),
(name school), (name school).
The name of my school is (name school),
That's the name of my school.
The name of my teacher is (name teacher),
(name teacher), (name teacher).
The name of my teacher is (name teacher),
That's the name of my teacher.

 SONGS & RHYMES

Howdy Neighbor

When?

Use this poem to gather children for circle time or story, or to get rid of wiggles any time during the day.

Why?

Children feel good when they say this poem. They will be sitting down and listening before they know it!

What?

No materials are needed.

How?

➤ Say this rhyme and perform the motions.

Howdy neighbor! (make big waving motion)
What do you say? (shake hands with each other)
It's going to be
A beautiful day. (make circle in front of body with arms)
So clap your hands, (clap your hands)
And stomp your feet. (stomp feet)
Jump up and down, (jump)
Then take a seat. (sit on the floor or in chairs)

Adaptation

➤ Here's a similar poem which lets children move and then sit down.

We step, step, step, (step in place)
And clap, clap, clap (clap)
And bow without a sound. (bow at waist)

We step, step, step, (step in place)
And clap, clap, clap (clap)
And then we touch the ground. (touch the floor)

We clap down low. (clap low)
We clap up high. (clap high in air)
We touch the ground. (touch the floor)
We touch the sky. (reach hands above head)

We step, step, step, (step in place)
And clap, clap, clap, (clap)
And then we sit right down. (sit down on the floor)

►►►►►►► SHARING ►►►►►►►

Show and Tell and Then Some

When?

Show and tell can be used as part of circle time or whenever there are a few extra minutes in the day.

Why?

Most children love to be the center of attention. Sharing with their friends in this way also gives them the opportunity to develop language skills and self-confidence.

What?

objects children bring from home

How?

Is Show and Tell dragging? Try one of these variations to liven it up.

► Only do Show and Tell on one designated day each week.

► Assign different children a special day each week when they can bring something to share.

► Encourage children to bring an object from nature or something they have made.

► Let other children in the room ask questions about the object brought in for Show and Tell.

► Have a sharing table where children place their items from Show and Tell for their classmates to look at and explore during the day. (Passing objects around the circle is usually very distracting and takes too long.)

► Make a Show and Tell bag or basket. Each night one child takes it home and brings in something the next day to share with the class.

► Relate Show and Tell to a theme or concept. For example, if the children are learning about tools, ask the children to bring in a tool; when discussing spring, request that the children bring in a sign of spring; if the children are learning about the color blue, then ask the children to bring in something blue.

► Rather than showing objects, let children tell jokes, riddles or retell favorite stories to the class.

 ▶▶▶▶▶▶ SHARING ▶▶▶▶▶▶

Thumbs Up—Whisper Up

When?

Thumbs up for this idea when every child in the room wants to shout at the same time.

Why?

This technique encourages children to think before saying the answer and helps them develop self-control. In addition, it gives children who might respond a little more slowly the opportunity to think.

What?

No materials are needed.

How?

▶ When asking the group a question, tell each child to hold up his thumb if he knows the answer.

▶ When all the children have had ample time to think about it and have their thumbs up, tell them to whisper the answer together.

▶ For example, count "1, 2, 3," and then let the children whisper the answer together.

Adaptations

▶ Tell children to "put your hands on your head," "touch your nose," "blink your eyes" and make other motions when they want to answer a question.

▶ Use "thinking partners" to encourage cooperative learning. Pair children, ask them to talk about a question and then answer it together.

 NAME SONGS

Sing a Name

When?

Name songs create positive feelings and are a wonderful way to start the day or circle time.

Why?

Young children love hearing their names sung. Name songs enhance children's self-esteem by making them feel special and an important part of the group.

What?

No materials are needed.

How?

▶ Sing the following song to the tune of "Row, Row, Row Your Boat."

▶ Insert a child's name.

▶ Sing to the children who are sitting quietly, or sing to get a child's attention and interest.

How, how, how do you do? (shake child's hand)
(Child's name), how are you?
I'm glad to say I'm fine today. (point to self)
I hope that you are, too. (point to child)

Adaptations

▶ Good Morning (Tune: "Did You Ever See a Lassie?")

Good morning to (child's name),
To (child's name), to (child's name),
Good morning to (child's name),
How do you do?

▶ We're All Here Today (Tune: "Farmer in the Dell")

We're all here today. (clap hands as you sing)
We're all here today.
Let's all clap together,
Because we're all here today.

(First child's name) is here today.
(Second child's name) is here today.
(Third child's name) is here today.
And (fourth child's name) is here today.

Continue singing until all the children are mentioned, then end the song by repeating the first verse.

▶ Here I Am (Tune: "Where Is Thumbkin?")

Where is (child's name)?
Where is (child's name)?
Here I am. Here I am. (child stands and sings)
How are you today (child's name)?
Very well, I thank you. (child responds)
Glad you're here.
Glad you're here.

▶▶▶▶▶▶▶   NAME SONGS   ▶▶▶▶▶▶▶

Get on Board

When?

This is a fun way to gather children for circle time or other large group activities.

Why?

Each child delights in having his name sung and will feel like a part of the group.

What?

No materials are needed.

How?

➤ Start chugging around the room like an engine.

➤ The children put their hands on each others' waists and make a train behind you.

➤ Sing the following song to the tune of "Little Liza Jane."

I have a friend that you all know
And (child's name) is his name. (children get
*   behind you when their names are sung)*
I have a friend that you all know
And (child's name) is his name.
Get on board little children.
Get on board little children.
Get on board little children.
There's room for many a more.

➤ When all the children are chugging along on the train, lead them over to the circle time area.

➤ Tell them to get off the train and have a seat.

Adaptations

➤ Give the child in the front of the train an engineer's hat to wear, then let the children play follow the leader around the room.

➤ Walk around the room taking children's hands to form a big circle, while singing the following song to the tune of "Skip to My Lou."

Friend, oh, friend, (walk up to a child)
How do you do? (hold out hands)
Both my hands (grasp hands)
I give to you.
Round we go, (walk in a circle holding hands)
Round and then
Off to find (go up to another child)
Another friend.

 NAME SONGS

Looking Through My Window

When?

Children enjoy using a prop to sing this name song.

Why?

This activity encourages friendships and promotes positive feelings of group acceptance.

What?

empty picture frame (8" x 12" works well) or matte board or poster board cut to look like a window

How?

► Look through the picture frame.

► Sing the following to the tune of "Go In and Out the Window."

I'm looking through my window.
   (look through picture frame)
I'm looking through my window.
I'm looking through my window.
And I see my friend (child's name).

► Pass the frame to the child whose name was mentioned in the song, then let that child look through the frame and say the name of another friend.

► Continue until everyone has had a turn.

Adaptation

► Change the words of the Bill Martin's story *Brown Bear, Brown Bear, What Do You See?*, using the children's names.

(First child), (first child), who do you see?
I see (second child) looking at me.

(Second child), (second child), who do you see?
I see (third child) looking at me., etc.

After every child's name has been said, end with:

Teacher, teacher, who do you see?
I see all my happy children smiling at me.

 NAME SONGS

Letter Song

When?

Use this song to start circle time or at other times in the day.

Why?

Letters are introduced in a meaningful way with this song.

What?

poster board or heavy paper
markers
scissors
clear contact paper

Preparation

► Cut the paper into 26 pieces 8-1/2" x 11".

► Print the letters of the alphabet on the cards. Laminate or cover with clear contact.

How?

► One child at a time stands in front of the group.

► Find the letter that her name starts with and let her hold up the letter.

► Sing the following to the tune of "C Is for Cookie."

T is for Tabitha, (insert letter and child's name in the song)
That's good enough for me.
T is for Tabitha,
That's good enough for me.
T is for Tabitha, (insert letter and child's name in the song)
That's good enough for me.
Oh, Tabitha, Tabitha, Tabitha,
Starts with T.

► Continue giving each child the letter that her name begins with, and singing the song to her.

Adaptations

► Ask the children to make letters with their bodies.

► Use the alphabet cards for other songs and games, or to dismiss the children from circle time. (For example, hold up a letter and if a child's name begins with that letter, she may go to a center.)

 NAME SONGS

I'll Find a Friend

When?

Start the day with this song or use it to change activities.

Why?

The activity encourages children to feel part of the group and develop social skills.

What?

No materials are needed.

How?

▶ Ask each child to find a friend to help him do the movements to the song.

▶ Sing the following to the tune of "Farmer in the Dell."

I'll find a friend at school. (two or three children get together and hold hands)
I'll find a friend at school.
I'm so glad I came today.
I'll find a friend at school.

We'll skip around the room... (children hold hands and skip)
We'll jump up and down... (children jump together)
We'll tiptoe around the room... (children tiptoe)

▶ Continue singing, adding other motions.

▶ End with this verse.

We'll sit down quietly. (sit down on rug)
We'll sit down quietly.
I'm so glad I have a friend.
We'll sit down quietly.

Adaptations

▶ Help shy children or other children who have difficulty finding a friend to play with to find a partner.

▶ Change the words of the last verse to direct the children to other activities such as "We'll line up to go outside" or "We'll wash our hands for lunch."

▶▶▶▶▶▶▶ CALENDAR ▶▶▶▶▶▶▶

Today Is Monday

Monday — Bread and Butter
Tuesday — String Beans
Wednesday — Soup
Thursday — Roast Beef
Friday — Fish
Saturday — Pizza
Sunday — Chicken

When?

Get children involved at circle time by singing this song.

Why?

This activity enhances auditory memory, sequencing skills and eye-hand coordination.

What?

poster board (seven pieces, each one 11" x 14")
markers, scissors, glue
food pictures from magazines, coupons, etc.
paper plates

Preparation

▶ Cut out food pictures of bread and butter, string beans, soup, roast beef, fish, pizza and chicken. Vary the kinds of food pictures to reflect foods with which the children are familiar.

▶ Glue the foods to the paper plates, then attach the paper plates to the poster board.

▶ Print the days of the week on the top of the poster board cards, and the name of the food on the bottom.

How?

▶ Pass the song cards out to seven children.

▶ Have them stand in the correct sequence in front of the group.

▶ As their food is mentioned in the song, they hold up their card.

▶ Sing the following to the tune of "She'll Be Coming 'Round the Mountain."

Today is Monday, shout hooray!
(cheer by raising hand)
Today is Monday, shout hooray!
We'll have bread and butter.
(clap hands on bread and butter)
We'll have bread and butter.
All you lucky children, that's okay.
...Tuesday...string beans...
(snap fingers on string beans)
...Wednesday...soup... (pretend to sip soup)
...Thursday...roast beef...
(pretend to cut meat)
...Friday...fish... (wiggle hand like a fish)
...Saturday...pizza...
(hold hand in air as if carrying a pizza)
...Sunday...chicken... (put hands under arm-
pits and flap arms like wings)

▶▶▶▶▶▶▶ CALENDAR ▶▶▶▶▶▶▶

What Shall We Do Today?

When?

Here's a song to start the day and give children something to look forward to.

Why?

This song encourages children to make plans each day as well as introduces them to the days of the week.

What?

classroom calendar

How?

▶ Choose a child to point to the date on the calendar.

▶ Sing the following to the tune of "Mary Had a Little Lamb."

What shall we do today,
Do today, do today?
Today is (day of the week)
So what shall we do today?

▶ Let the children suggest various things they'd like to do such as finger paint, sing songs, build with blocks, play outside, etc. Then add them to the song. For example:

We'll play outside today,
Outside today, outside today.
Today is (day of the week)
And we'll play outside today.

Adaptations

▶ Write a language experience story about what the children plan to do that day.

▶ Let the children make journals. They draw pictures, then dictate sentences about what they want to do each day.

▶ Make a large daily schedule, then go over it with the children. Talk about all the things planned for the day.

 CALENDAR

Seven Days in the Week

When?

Here's another song to sing while doing calendar activities at circle time.

Why?

Children learn about the days of the week and sequential ordering.

What?

No materials are needed.

How?

▶ Sing the song below to the tune of "The Bear Went Over the Mountain."

▶ Count the days of the week on fingers or point to the words on the calendar.

There are seven days in the week, (hold up seven fingers)
Seven days in the week,
Seven days in the week,
And I can name each one.

There is Sunday, Monday and Tuesday, (hold up a finger for each day as you sing)
Wednesday, Thursday and Friday.
The last day is Saturday,
And I have named each one.

Adaptations

Learn the days of the week with these tunes.

▶ "Zippity Doo Dah" (Traditional Tune)

Zippity doo dah, zippity ay. (clap hands as you sing)
My, oh, my what a wonderful day!
Plenty of sunshine heading my way.
Zippity doo dah, zippity ay.

Sunday, Monday, Tuesday, Wednesday,
Thursday, Friday and Saturday.
Sunday, Monday, Tuesday, Wednesday,
Thursday, Friday and Saturday.

▶ "Mulberry Bush" (Traditional Tune)

This is the way we wash our clothes, (act out motions for the days as you sing)
Wash our clothes, wash our clothes.
This is the way we wash our clothes,
So early Monday morning.
Tuesday—iron clothes
Wednesday—sweep the floor
Thursday—mend the clothes
Friday—bake the bread
Saturday—scrub the floor
Sunday—skip and play

▶ Let children make up their own verses and motions for things they can do each day.

▶▶▶▶▶▶▶ CALENDAR ▶▶▶▶▶▶▶

Yesterday, Today & Tomorrow

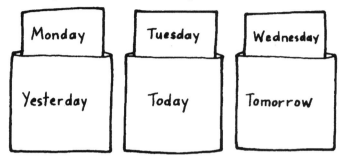

When?

Use this activity to review what the children did yesterday and to plan for the new day.

Why?

Time is a concept that is very abstract for young children. This daily chart introduces days of the week in a meaningful way and encourages children to make plans.

What?

3 large envelopes
12" x 24" poster board
glue
markers
7 index cards, 4" x 6"

Preparation

▶ Cut off the tops of the envelopes, then glue them to the poster board to make pockets. Write yesterday, today and tomorrow on the envelopes.

▶ Print a day of the week on the top of each index card.

How?

▶ After referring to the classroom calendar and talking about the date, place the appropriate cards in the envelopes saying, "Yesterday was (name day of week). Today is (name day of week). Tomorrow will be (name day of week)."

▶ Ask the children to share what they did in school yesterday, then ask them to say what they plan to do today.

▶ Build anticipation and interest by planning something special for tomorrow.

Adaptations

▶ Use this activity at the end of the day to help children recall what they learned and to build excitement for the coming day.

▶ Choose a child to be the calendar helper. This child places the appropriate cards in the envelopes.

▶▶▶▶▶▶ CALENDAR ▶▶▶▶▶▶

Weather Watch

When?

This routine adds learning to circle time.

Why?

Weather activities encourage children to observe nature and make predictions.

What?

12" square of poster board
crayons or markers
construction paper
brad fastener
scissors
yarn
hole punch

Preparation

▶ Divide the poster board into four sections and draw symbols for major types of weather. Use symbols that are relevant to your region of the country.

▶ Cut a small arrow from construction paper and attach it to the center of the weather chart with the brad fastener.

▶ Punch two holes at the top and hang with yarn.

How?

▶ Select a weather person, and ask her to stand in the front of the room.

▶ Sing the following song to the tune of "Shortnin' Bread."

What will the weather, weather, weather?
What will the weather person say?
(Child's name) says it's (weather), (insert the word rainy, sunny, snowy, cloudy, cold, etc.)
(weather), (weather).
(Child's name) says it's (weather),
(Weather) today.

Adaptations

▶ Let children make their own weather charts to use at home.

▶ Keep a monthly graph of the different types of weather.

▶ Put a rain gauge or thermometer on the playground for the children to observe and record rainfall and temperatures.

▶ Here's another weather song to the tune of "B-I-N-G-O."

There is some weather in the sky,
and Rainy is its name-o.
R-A-I-N-Y, R-A-I-N-Y, R-A-I-N-Y,
And Rainy is its name-o.
(Insert snowy, windy, etc.)

Dress Me

When?

Use this activity at circle time along with the weather song.

Why?

Children learn how to make decisions about what to wear when they go outside.

What?

basket or clothes tree
children's clothing and accessories for different types of weather

Preparation

➤ Collect boots, an umbrella, sun hat, stocking cap, mittens, sandals, sweater, coat, etc. Look in the school's "Lost and Found," or ask parents to send in items that their children have outgrown.

➤ Hang the items on the clothes tree or put them in the basket.

How?

➤ After the weather report, ask the children what kind of clothes they think they will need when they go out to play.

➤ Let one child select the appropriate clothes from the basket and hold them up.

➤ After play time, discuss their prediction and whether or not it was appropriate.

Adaptations

➤ Make a small boy and small girl from felt. Cut out felt clothing for them for different types of weather. For example, mittens, rain hat, shorts, jacket, etc. Let children take turns picking out clothes and dressing the felt children for the weather.

➤ Have a news show with news reporters and a weather forecaster. Include school news, the lunch menu, weather, etc.

➤ Ask children to bring in weather maps from the newspaper or listen to the weather report on the television or radio.

▶▶▶▶▶▶▶ CALENDAR ▶▶▶▶▶▶▶

Math Fun

When?

Take advantage of a teachable moment by incorporating math concepts with the calendar at circle time.

Why?

Math understanding begins with everyday experiences in counting, patterning, graphing, numeral recognition and time.

What?

large calendar (Indicate children's birthdays, field trips and other special events on the calendar.)

Cut out numerals and seasonal shapes to fit in the daily boxes of the calendar, for example, fall—apples, leaves, acorns; winter—sleds, snowflakes, holiday symbols; spring—flowers, umbrellas, birds; summer—suns, pails/shovels, stars, etc.

How?

▶ Choose one child each day to come to the front of the room and add a shape or numeral to the calendar in the appropriate box.

▶ Then use the activities below, adapting them to the needs and abilities of your children.

• Count the days, pointing to each numeral and sweeping your hand from left to right.

• Count the days until special events, like birthdays or parties.

• Make a pattern from the cutout shapes. For example, alternate green and red apples or orange and yellow leaves. Ask, "What do you think the color of the next apple will be?"

• Say the days of the week as you point to them.

• Introduce the months of the year.

• Count the number of children present and write it on the calendar each day. Use these figures to make comparisons such as "Were more children here yesterday or today?"

• Graph the number of children at school each day.

• Cut squares of paper the size of the sections on the calendar. Let one child each day color a picture of what he is looking forward to doing at school that day, then hang it on the calendar.

 YOU'RE SPECIAL

Tony Chestnut

When?

Sing "Tony Chestnut" at circle time or whenever a child needs a little love.

Why?

It's been said that people don't care how much you know until they know how much you care. That's particularly true for young children, who can't hear often enough how much they are loved.

What?

No materials are needed.

How?

➤ Point to parts of the body while singing the following song to the tune of "London Bridge."

Tony (point to toe and then knee)
Chestnut (point to chest, then head)
Knows (touch nose)
I (touch eye)
Love (cross hands over chest)
You, (point to a child)
Knows I love you, (continue with the motions above)
Knows I love you.
Tony Chestnut
Knows I love you.
Tony knows.

Adaptations

➤ Catch children doing the right thing and reinforce the behavior by singing the following song to the tune of "Skip to My Lou."

If your name is (child's name)
I like you!
If your name is (child's name)
I like you!
If your name is (child's name)
I like you!
And I hope you like me, too!

➤ Make a language experience chart where the children dictate the end to this sentence, "I like myself because..." or "I like (another child) because..."

▶▶▶▶▶▶   YOU'RE SPECIAL   ▶▶▶▶▶▶

Little Red Box

When?

Here's a song to start the day on a positive note and make children feel very special.

Why?

Little Red Box reinforces children's self-esteem and encourages name recognition.

What?

shoe box or cardboard food box
red paper
glue or tape
scissors
markers
index cards or heavy paper cut into 4" x 6"
    pieces—one for each child
photographs of children

Preparation

▶ Cover the box with red paper.

▶ Print each child's name on an index card and put it in the box. If photographs of the children are available, glue them onto the cards.

How?

▶ One at a time, pull children's names out of the red box while singing the following song to the tune of "Polly Wolly Doodle."

I wish I had a little red box
    (pull out name card)
To put my (child's name) in.
I'd take her out
And go "How do you do?" (shake hands)
And put her back again. (put card back
    in box)

Adaptations

▶ Cover a large cardboard box with red paper and let children take turns crawling in and out of the box while singing the song.

▶ To start the day, go up to each child, look her in the eyes, sing the song and hug her and say, "I'd take you out and go hug, hug, hug, and put you back again."

▶ Let children name other family members and pretend to take them out of the box and kiss and hug them as they sing.

▶ Change the color of the box to match what the child is wearing. For example, if Amy were wearing yellow, sing, "I wish I had a little yellow box to put my Amy in. I'd take her out and go 'How do you do?' and put her back again."

YOU'RE SPECIAL

I Am Special!

When?

Children will quickly join circle time when you sing this song to them.

Why?

This activity helps children feel good about themselves and focuses on their positive characteristics.

What?

hand mirror

How?

▶ Begin by singing the following song to the tune of "Frere Jacques" to the whole group.

You are special,
You are special.
Take a look
You will see.
Someone very special,
Someone very special.
And it's you!
And it's you!

▶ Next, pass the mirror around and sing the second verse to each child individually while she looks in the mirror.

I am special,
I am special.
Take a look
You will see.
Someone very special,
Someone very special.
And it's me!
And it's me!

▶ Ask each child to say something special about herself before passing the mirror to the next person.

Adaptations

▶ Glue a small mirror inside a box with a lid. Tell the children the most wonderful thing in the whole world is in the box, then let them open it and see what it is!

▶ Have children look in a mirror (or make play mirrors by covering cardboard with aluminum foil) as they say

I looked at the mirror
And what did I see?
A beautiful child
Just smiling at me!

 YOU'RE SPECIAL ▶▶▶▶▶▶▶

Me

When?

Say this poem to quiet children for circle time or use it throughout the day as a little pick-me-up.

Why?

Children feel worthy and capable when they get lots of positive feedback.

What?

No materials are needed.

How?

▶ Ask the children to repeat each line of the poem after you.

> I've got ten little fingers, (hold up ten fingers)
> And ten little toes, (point to feet)
> Two little eyes, (point to eyes)
> A mouth (point to mouth)
> And a nose. (touch nose)
> Put them all together, (put hands on hips)
> And what have you got?
> You've got me, my friend, (point to self)
> And that's a lot! (hug self)

Adaptations

▶ Periodically during the day, tell the children to give themselves a hug and say, "I'm pretty special."

▶ Have children make a book called "All about Me." They could draw a self-portrait on one page, and on other pages put a family picture, pictures of their pets, friends, what they like to do at school, favorite foods, favorite books, etc.

▶ Cover a large detergent box or coffee can. Write "Me" on it and decorate it with glitter and stars. Each day let one child take the can or box home and fill it with special objects that they like. They bring it to school the next day and share the contents with the other children.

 YOU'RE SPECIAL

We Like You

When?

Faces will light up when circle time (or anytime!) starts with this activity.

Why?

This activity reinforces positive social behaviors, as well as children's self-esteem and language skills.

What?

sentence strips or 3" x 5" index cards
markers
masking tape
can

Preparation

► Discuss what it means to be a friend. Have the children dictate words that describe good friends. For example, great, kind, nice, helpful, shares, etc.

► Print one word on each sentence strip or index card, then place all the words in the can. Make enough words so there will be one for each child in the room.

How?

► One at a time, let a child come up and choose a word from the can.

► Tape the word to the child while singing the following to the tune of "We Wish You a Merry Christmas."

We like you because you're (insert word).
We like you because you're (insert word).
We like you because you're (insert word).
We really like you!

Adaptations

► During the day ask children if they remember what their word says and if they are remembering to act that way?

► Think of an adjective that begins with the same letter as the child's name, for example, Terrific Tabitha, Friendly Franco or Wonderful William.

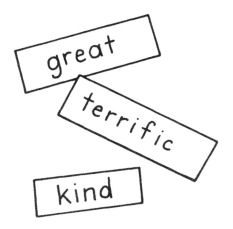

If You're Happy

When?

This familiar song is a good one for circle time and at other busy times to focus children's attention.

Why?

Children learn the names of parts of the body, as well as how to express different emotions and feelings.

What?

construction paper
scissors, markers, glue
yarn
wiggly eyes
popsicle sticks

Preparation

► Cut six 3" circles from the construction paper.

► Draw expressions similar to those shown, then decorate with markers, yarn hair, wiggly eyes, etc.

► Glue or tape the circles to the sticks.

How?

► Give one puppet to each of six children.

► Each child holds up her puppet for the appropriate verse.

► Everyone sings.

> If you're happy and you know it clap your hands.
> If you're happy and you know it clap your hands.
> If you're happy and you know it,
> Then your face will surely show it.
> If you're happy and you know it clap your hands.

> If you're sad—rub your eyes. (pretend to cry)
> If you're mad—stomp your feet. (stomp feet)
> If you're scared—shiver and shake. (shake)
> If you're surprised—say "Oh, my!" (say "Oh, my!")
> If you're sleepy—close your eyes. (close eyes)

Adaptations

► Ask the children what makes them feel angry, sad, happy, etc.

► What do you do when you get angry?

► What do you do when you're afraid?

 **YOU'RE SPECIAL** ▶▶▶▶▶▶▶

We All Think You're Wonderful

When?

Here's a positive way to start circle time or give children a boost when they're having a difficult day.

Why?

This activity encourages children to look for the best in themselves and others.

What?

No materials are needed.

How?

▶ Have the children sit in a circle.

▶ Choose one child at a time to stand in the middle as everyone chants the following to the tune of "Dry Bones."

We all think you're wonderful, (slap thighs and clap hands to the beat)
We do.
We give a lot of credit
To you.
We all think that (child's name)
Is true blue.
We shout our praises to you,
We do!

▶ Encourage the other children to tell the child in the middle of the circle what they like about him. Each day choose another child. Keep this activity in circle time until all of the children have had a turn.

Adaptations

▶ Make a mailbox for each child from a cereal box. Provide materials for the children at the art center or writing center so they can draw pictures and letters for their friends.

▶ Divide children into pairs and let them draw pictures of each other. Ask them to share these with the other children and tell something new they learned about their friends.

▶ Engage children in making murals, posters and other cooperative learning activities.

▶▶▶▶▶▶ YOU'RE SPECIAL ▶▶▶▶▶▶

I Like Myself

When?

Use this chant to get children's attention when starting circle time or changing activities.

Why?

Young children are very egocentric. This chant teaches about parts of the body while building positive feelings of self.

What?

No materials are needed.

How?

▶ Ask the children to repeat each line of the chant and perform the actions.

I like myself. (give self a hug)
I'm glad I'm me. (big smile)
I like my nose. (point to nose)
I like my toes. (touch toes)
I like my shoulders. (rub shoulders)
I like my back. (pat back)
I like my ears. (touch ears)

▶ Continue with other parts of the body. End with this line.

I like all of me! Yeah! (clap and cheer)

Adaptations

▶ Let children make up their own lines for what they like about themselves.

▶ Make a language experience chart of this chant for children to follow along.

▶ Have children draw pictures of and dictate sentences about what they like about themselves. Put the pictures together to make a book for the class called "I Like Myself."

▶▶▶▶▶▶ YOU'RE SPECIAL ▶▶▶▶▶▶

Happy, Happy Birthday!

When?

Celebrate each child's birthday with a song, cheer and some special attention.

Why?

Birthdays are an exciting time for little ones, and these activities will add to their happy memories.

What?

construction paper
glitter
stickers
scissors
glue
markers
stapler

Preparation

▶ Cut out a paper crown and fit it around the child's head.

▶ Let the birthday child decorate it with glitter, stickers and markers.

How?

▶ At circle time, have the birthday child sit in a special place such as a decorated chair, the center of the circle or the teacher's lap.

▶ Sing the traditional song to the birthday child.

Happy birthday to you,
Happy birthday to you,
Happy birthday dear (child's name),
Happy birthday to you.
How old are you?
How old are you?
How old is dear (child's name)?
How old are you?

▶ Together clap out the number of years old the child is. End with, "and wishes for many, many more," while clapping rapidly. Say three cheers for the birthday girl. "Hip-hip-hooray! Hip-hip-hooray! Hip-hip-hooray!"

Adaptations

▶ Give the birthday girl a special wish at school for her birthday. Children often wish for simple things such as to ride the tricycle, to sit next to the teacher at lunch, to play a certain game, etc.

▶ Make a button or badge for the birthday child to wear.

▶ Make a birthday book for the child. Let classmates draw pictures, then put them together with a construction paper cover which the birthday child gets to decorate.

Terrific Teaching Props

When?

Concrete objects are the gateway to learning and understanding for young children and should be used when presenting new concepts, themes and other information.

Why?

Props, pictures, toys and sensory materials are essential tools for children's learning.

What?

Capture children's interest with these props and objects and encourage them to explore and experiment with many different materials.

▶ **Toys**—Toys are a natural stepping stone to learning. Toys from other countries and homemade toys, as well as toys made from natural materials, are particularly interesting for children.

▶ **Animals**—Live animals, whenever available, provide delightful learning opportunities. Children will often find little critters to bring to class, or ask parents, veterinarians, animal shelters and others to bring in animals.

▶ **Natural Objects**—The world is full of beautiful things to gather. Leaves, rocks, shells, dirt, seeds, nuts and flowers are but a few of Mother Nature's treasures that can be used to spark a conversation, for math activities and to enliven many other classroom experiences.

▶ **Books**—Positive attitudes about reading are nurtured when books are used at circle time and at other times throughout the day. Books not only entertain children, but also take them to new places and give them new experiences, words and ideas.

▶ **Junk**—See something interesting in the trash can? What can you do with an empty cardboard box, packing materials, plastic lids or advertising displays? Keep your eyes and ears open and recycle "good junk" in the classroom to build, sort, make inventions, do art projects, etc. Ask parents to save things from home and work.

▶ **Maps, Globes, Brochures, Tools**—Anything that adults use is of great interest to children. Allow them to manipulate, explore, take apart and put back together a variety of things.

▶▶▶▶▶▶▶   TEACHING PROPS   ▶▶▶▶▶▶▶

Sensory Starters

When?

Set the stage for learning by stimulating children's senses.

Why?

Children learn by smelling, hearing, touching, tasting and seeing. Indeed, think of each sense as a pathway to learning and engage as many as possible when teaching young children.

What?

Here are just a few ideas for challenging children's senses in order to get them interested in a particular topic or concept.

▶ **Smell**—Hide a popcorn popper under a box. Turn it on secretly and notice children's reactions. What a fun way to introduce the day's snack!

Put a slice of lemon, a pickle, peanut butter, bubble gum, coffee, peppermint abstract, Italian seasoning and other items with distinguishable smells in the bottom of baby food jars or film containers. Punch small holes in the lids and let children try to identify the objects by smell.

▶ **Hear**—Play a musical instrument from another country. Talk about how the instrument was made, as well as the culture from which it originated.

Make different animal sounds (or use a toy that makes sounds) to introduce a theme on farm animals, pets or wild animals.

▶ **Taste**—Pass around small samples of bagels, pita bread, cornbread, french bread, tortillas and other types of bread. Talk about foods from different cultures.

▶ **Touch**—Place an object in a sock and tie a knot at the top. Pass it around and let the children try to identify it from touch. Hide an object in your pocket or a sack.

Put a variety of leaves in a basket (big, little, rough, smooth, soft, prickly, etc.). Let the children feel them and describe them.

  **TEACHING PROPS**

Guessing Jar

When?

The Guessing Jar is interesting anytime, or it can be used with a particular theme or holiday by simply varying the contents.

Why?

The Guessing Jar invites participation and gives children hands-on experience with estimating and counting.

What?

clear plastic jar or container
small objects (plastic toys, math counters, natural objects like rocks or shells, coins, discarded objects, common classroom items like crayons)

How?

➤ Place a number of objects in the jar and put the jar in a prominent place in the room before the children arrive.

➤ At circle time, pass the jar around and let each child guess how many objects are in it.

➤ Pour the contents of the jar on the floor and count how many there are.

➤ Did anyone guess the correct number? Who thought there were more? Who thought there were less?

Adaptations

➤ Use the objects for sorting, classifying and other math experiences.

➤ On a large chart, write each child's name and his estimate.

➤ Give each child one of the objects from the jar to hold and explore. Talk about how it feels, smells, etc. Ask open-ended questions such as "What can you do with it?" "Where does it come from?"

➤ For a classroom party, fill the guessing jar with treats for the children.

Mystery Box

When?

Put this box in the middle of the room to spark children's curiosity when they come to school in the morning, or use it at circle time to introduce a new concept or theme.

Why?

Children need hands-on experiences with concrete objects that they can see, hear and touch. They also need opportunities to ask questions, organize information and hypothesize.

What?

shoe box, detergent box or similar box with a top

gold or silver spray paint

toy, object from nature, tool, sensory object, item relating to a theme or concept, instrument, book, etc.

Preparation

▶ Spray paint the box gold or silver. Decorate it, if desired.

▶ Place one object inside the box. Tape the box closed or tie a ribbon around it so they don't "peek."

How?

▶ At circle time, pass the mystery box around the circle and let the children guess what is inside.

▶ Let them ask questions about what is in the box or give them clues.

▶ After everyone has had an opportunity to ask questions or guess what is inside, open the box and take out the mystery object.

Adaptations

▶ Use stacking boxes or bags of varying sizes. Hide a teaching prop in the smallest one. Build anticipation as the children remove one box at a time and try to guess what is inside.

▶ Let the children take turns bringing home the mystery box and finding a special object around their house to put in it. When they come to school the next day, the other children guess what is inside, or the child gives them hints about it.

 TEACHING PROPS

Hats and Costumes

When?

Surprise children by wearing a costume or hat to encourage their curiosity and thinking skills.

Why?

Hats and costumes spark children's interest.

What?

hats (from various careers, cultures, sports, for different types of weather, etc.)
clothing, props

How?

▶ Before children arrive in the morning or before group time, put on a hat or costume.

▶ Play a guessing game such as "Who am I?" "What do I do?" "What time of year is it?"

▶ Use the costume to stimulate questions and discussion with the children.

Adaptations

▶ Read a story, have a guest speaker or take a field trip related to the clothing.

▶ Let children play with the hats and costumes in the housekeeping area.

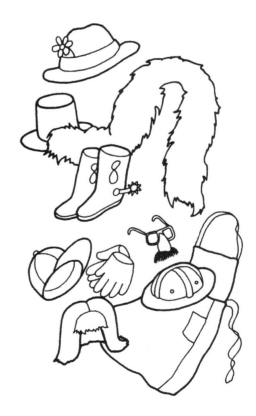

 TEACHING PROPS

Stand-Up Animals

When?

Stand-up animals are great fun at circle time, story time or anytime.

Why?

Props focus children's attention and the children can play with them.

What?

cardboard rolls (from toilet paper or paper towel)
construction paper
scissors
markers
glue

Preparation

➤ Color and cut out animals that are approximately 5" tall from construction paper.

➤ Glue or tape the animals to cardboard rolls.

How?

➤ Hide the stand-up animals in your lap or in a bag or box.

➤ Pull them out and place them on the floor as you tell a story, sing a song or introduce a new theme.

Adaptations

➤ Create characters and props for children to use in retelling a story.

➤ Let children draw their own animals and use buttons, yarn, wiggly eyes and fabric scraps to decorate them.

  **TEACHING PROPS**

Coat Hanger Critter

When?

Coat hanger puppets are a fun way to introduce new themes or concepts or to give children directions.

Why?

Children enjoy listening to puppets and making up stories with puppets.

What?

coat hanger
old nylon stockings
cloth tape
yarn, felt scraps, buttons, wiggly eyes, etc.
scissors
glue

Preparation

► Stretch the hanger into a diamond shape as shown, then pull the stocking over it and tie at the bottom.

► Bend the hook into an oval and tape it in place so it won't poke the children.

► Decorate the puppet to look like one of the characters shown or create your own critters.

How?

► Hold up the puppet and ask the children to guess its name.

► When a child says a name that suits the puppet, say, "Yes, you're right. How did you know?"

► Next, let the puppet tell the children a story, share a new theme, give directions for a new game or activity, etc.

Adaptation

► Children will enjoy making their own coat hanger puppets to use in dramatizing stories or singing songs.

Oh, Henry!

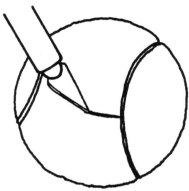

When?

Let Henry start the day by saying good morning to the children or use him to introduce new activities.

Why?

Young children look forward to having Henry as part of their daily opening ritual.

What?

box with a lid
tennis ball
sharp knife
wiggly eyes, pompom, yarn
glue
markers

Preparation

► Using a sharp knife, cut a slit between two seams on the tennis ball for a mouth. (An adult will need to do this.)

► Add eyes, a pompom nose, yarn hair and a big smile.

How?

► Put the ball puppet in the box.

► Knock on the lid and say, "Oh, Henry. Oh, Henry, the boys and girls want to say good morning to you."

► Open the lid of the box and pull out Henry.

► Squeeze the sides of the ball to make his mouth move as he says, "Good morning, friends."

► Then let Henry speak to each child or ask him questions about what he wants to do that day.

Adaptations

► Create other animals and characters from tennis balls to use for stories, songs and language activities.

► Decorate a gift box or detergent box, then cut a hole in the back that your arm can go through. Put a tennis ball puppet or hand puppet in the box, insert your hand in the hole and make the puppet pop up and talk to the children.

 **TEACHING PROPS**

Stick Puppets

When?

Children enjoy holding and playing with their own stick puppets at circle time.

Why?

These puppets give each child something concrete to hold in her hands and manipulate.

What?

construction paper
popsicle sticks or plastic straws
tape
scissors
markers or crayons

Preparation

▶ Using a theme, shape, color, animal or object of interest to the children, cut out a little puppet for each child. (See illustrations.)

▶ Tape the puppets to straws or sticks and let the children decorate with markers or crayons. Store puppets in a can or basket.

How?

▶ Pass out a puppet to each child at circle time.

▶ After a few minutes of free play with the puppets, tell a story or sing a song with them.

▶ Use the puppets to motivate a class discussion, reinforce positional words or practice following directions. For example, "Put the puppet beside you." "Put the puppet on your shoulder." "Put the puppet under your chair."

Adaptation

▶ Have children cut out people from catalogs or magazines and tape to sticks to make puppets.

Picture Talk

When?

Pictures can be used to introduce a new concept or theme, or to extend a conversation.

Why?

This activity enhances children's reading readiness skills such as visual discrimination and visual memory.

What?

magazines, brochures, posters, calendars, greeting cards, newspapers, advertisements, photographs, etc.
file folders
construction paper
scissors
glue
clear contact paper

Preparation

▶ Collect pictures of toys, food, places, animals, people from many cultures, cars, homes and other things children are interested in.

▶ Mount the pictures on construction paper and laminate or cover with clear contact, if desired. File in folders according to themes, seasons, etc.

How?

▶ Place a picture face down in your lap, then slowly show it to the children.

▶ Ask open-ended questions such as "What do you see?" "What do you think the people are saying to each other?" "How do you think they feel?"

▶ Let the children make up a story about the picture, or ask them to think of a title for the picture.

▶ Place the picture face down in your lap. Ask the children to recall details in the picture. For example, "How many children were there?" "What color was the bird's tail?", etc.

Adaptations

▶ Cut several large holes in a large envelope. Place a picture in the envelope and play a guessing game to see who can identify the picture by what can be seen through the holes. Slowly pull it from the envelope to reveal the entire picture.

▶ Using postcards or calendar pictures of art masterpieces for discussion helps foster aesthetic appreciation in children.

 TEACHING PROPS ▶▶▶▶▶▶▶

Pass the Parcel

When?

Use Pass the Parcel to create excitement about a new theme, color, shape or numeral.

Why?

Children love surprises and will be delighted to find a surprise in the parcel.

What?

small box
object relating to a theme, story, color or other concept
tissue paper or newspaper and tape
music box, tape recorder or record player

Preparation

▶ Hide the object in the box.

▶ Wrap different layers of tissue paper or newspaper around the box. Wrap one layer for each child in the class.

How?

▶ Have the children sit in a circle.

▶ Tell them to pass the package or "parcel" around the circle when the music starts.

▶ When the music stops, whoever is holding the package may unwrap one layer. If the music stops on a person who has already had a turn, they may pass it to a friend on either side of them who has not yet had a turn.

▶ Continue passing the parcel until all the layers of paper have been removed, and all the children have had a chance to remove one layer.

▶ Open the box and see the surprise!

Adaptation

▶ Play Pass the Parcel as a fun party game by hiding little treats or prizes in the box (or under each layer of paper) for each child.

CLEAN-UP

Children will follow you like the Pied Piper when you turn clean-up time into a game. A "gentle touch" and encouragement are more successful than an authoritarian approach. If you hear moans and groans when you tell the children it's time to stop and pick up, try warning them ahead of time with one of the songs or techniques in this chapter. Besides helping children develop responsibility and respect for school materials, clean-up time can be a fun routine and transition.

As with other behaviors, a powerful technique to get children to clean up is to model what you want them to do. You might ask, "Do you need some help putting away the blocks?" Or give children a choice, "Would you like to tuck in the babies while I put away the dishes?" Whistle (or sing) while you work. Ask for their advice, "Where does this airplane belong?" Catch children doing the right thing and use verbal cues such as "William, I like the way you're putting the books away so neatly."

Other statements which encourage cooperation are also helpful such as "We'll have more time to play outside since we're all working together and helping each other."

When most of the children are through picking up, sit down on the floor and begin a story or finger play to focus their attention. If a second teacher is in the room, he or she can assist the stragglers and guide them to the next activity.

 CLEAN-UP SONGS

Tidy-Up

When?

Sing this tune to the children when it's time to clean up.

Why?

Children respond more readily to a pleasant song than to demanding statements.

What?

No materials are needed.

How?

▶ While putting away toys, begin singing this song to the tune of "Jingle Bells."

Tidy-up, tidy-up, put the toys away.
Tidy-up, tidy-up, we're finished for today.
Oh, tidy-up, tidy-up, put the toys away.
For we'll get them out again
The next time that we play.

Adaptations

▶ Let one child be the "singer" and skip around the room as he sings the clean-up song and reminds his friends what to do.

▶ Here are other helper songs to sing.

"A Helper I Will Be" (Tune: "Farmer in the Dell")

A helper I will be.
A helper I will be.
There's work to do,
There's work to do,
A helper I will be.

A picker-up I'll be, etc.

"Jolly Good Helper" (Tune: "For He's a Jolly Good Fellow")

(Child's name) is a jolly good helper. (insert
the names of children who are helping)
(Child's name) is a jolly good helper.
(Child's name) is a jolly good helper.
And (another child's name) is a helper, too.

▶▶▶▶▶▶▶   CLEAN-UP SONGS   ▶▶▶▶▶▶▶

Time for Clean-Up

When?

This song reminds children that it's clean-up time and gets them involved in the task.

Why?

Positive verbal cues encourage children to work together.

What?

No materials are needed.

How?

▶ Sing the following song to the tune of "Frere Jacques."

▶ Have the children echo each line of this song.

Time for clean-up. (children repeat)
Everyone. (children repeat)
Put the toys away. (children repeat)
Join the fun. (children repeat)

Adaptations

▶ Change the words of this song to communicate other things you want the children to do. For example, "Time for snack," or "Time to line up," or "Time for story."

▶ Another song to encourage the children to work together is the following, sung to the tune of "The Wheels on the Bus."

Come on everybody, it's clean-up time,
Clean-up time, clean-up time.
Come on everybody, it's clean-up time,
Clean up now.

 **CLEAN-UP SONGS**

Art Parade

When?

Have an art parade when children complete an art project. Then only a few minutes are needed to finish putting things away.

Why?

Children love to "show off" their artwork and will have fun marching around the room.

What?

record or tape with a bouncy beat

How?

▶ Tell the children they are going to have an art parade so everyone can see their pictures.

▶ Let them get their paintings, collages, puppets or whatever they have made.

▶ Help them pick up the art area while they get their artwork.

▶ Choose a leader and have the others get in line.

▶ Play the music as the children march around the room holding up their pictures.

Adaptations

▶ Visit other classrooms and show them your parade of art, or visit the school office or cafeteria.

▶ Let children take turns telling the other children the title of their artwork and describing how they made it.

 CLEAN-UP TOOLS

Timer

When?

A timer helps children bring closure to their activities and encourages them to participate in clean-up time.

Why?

Time has little meaning for children, but a five minute warning helps them feel more prepared and responsible.

What?

timer

How?

▶ Set the timer for five minutes.

▶ Remind children that when the timer goes off it will be time to finish playing and clean up.

▶ When the timer goes off, sing one of the clean-up songs.

▶ Start cleaning up, and the children will, too.

Adaptations

▶ Use a three minute sand glass instead of a timer. Begin singing when the sand has all run down.

▶ Use the timer to help children share toys. For example, set the timer for ten minutes for children to swing, ride a tricycle, play with a particularly popular toy, etc.

▶ Play "beat the clock" with the timer. Set it for five or ten minutes and see if the children can "beat the clock" by cleaning up and sitting down quietly for a story before the timer goes off.

▶ For older children who have difficulty staying with the task, let them use a timer and try to complete an activity in a given period of time.

Puppet Pals and Inspectors

When?

Check to see if everything is in its place with a puppet pal or inspector.

Why?

Children enjoy taking responsibility for making sure the room is cleaned properly. In addition, giving children responsibility empowers them and makes the classroom less authoritarian.

What?

hand puppet or stuffed animal

How?

▶ When children are just about through cleaning up, put the puppet on your hand and let the puppet go around the room and inspect various centers.

▶ Talk in the voice of the puppet, or let the puppet pretend to whisper in your ear and repeat what it says to the class.

▶ Give positive comments such as "Puppet pal likes the way all the puzzles have been put together," or a reminder like, "Puppet pal sees some blocks we need to put on the shelf."

▶ After modeling what to do with the puppet, let the children take turns using it to inspect the room and give feedback to the other children.

Adaptations

▶ Make a badge for the inspector. Give the child a note pad to "write down" what needs to be done.

▶ Assign a child to be "playground inspector." The inspector goes around and checks to see if all the toys have been put away after play.

 **CLEAN-UP TOOLS**

Masking Tape Machine

When?

Use this clean-up tool for a quick clean-up.

Why?

Tape is sticky, it's fun and it will make cleaning the floor a game.

What?

masking tape

How?

► Give each child a piece of masking tape (approximately 6" long).

► Show them how to wrap it around their fingers with the sticky side out.

► Tell them they're going to be vacuum cleaners and pick up the trash on the floor with their tape.

► Pretend to turn them "on" and make a humming sound like a vacuum cleaner.

► When the floor is picked up, turn them "off" and have them throw their tape in the trash.

Adaptations

► Child-size brooms are perfect for sweeping floors and sidewalks, and small carpet sweepers are great for cleaning rugs.

► A dust buster, or child-sized dust pans and brushes, are other useful classroom tools.

 CLEAN-UP TOOLS

Super Socks

When?

Old socks become new toys for children when it's time to clean.

Why?

Socks are "super" fun, fantastic dust-busters!

What?

old socks (one for each child)
basket

How?

▶ Put old socks in a basket.

▶ Ask the children to choose one and put it on their hand.

▶ Show each child how to dust the room and pick up the toys with her sock.

Adaptations

▶ Let children find the person who has a sock that matches theirs and sit down next to them.

▶ Put old socks on over shoes and "skate around the room."

▶ Have a clean-up day when the children wear old clothes and bring sponges, cloths and other cleaning tools. This is especially fun when the weather is warm.

▶ Let the children wash dolls, doll clothes and other plastic toys at the water table. Place them on drying racks or clothes lines to dry.

 CLEAN-UP TOOLS

Labels and Outlines

When?

Labels help children put materials back in their proper place.

Why?

Visual matching and sorting skills are reinforced with these picture clues, outlines and words.

What?

sentence strips or heavy paper
construction paper
markers
crayons
scissors
tape or clear contact

Preparation

▶ Write the names of classroom toys and materials on the sentence strips or paper.

▶ Draw picture clues or the outline of the item next to the words.

▶ Tape labels to shelves, tubs, boxes or containers. Cover with clear contact, if desired.

How?

▶ Demonstrate how to put the toys and tools where they belong by looking at the word and picture.

▶ Gather several toys and items from around the classroom.

▶ Let the children play "detective" and see if they can find where things belong.

Adaptations

▶ Use pictures from the boxes that toys come in to make labels, or cut pictures of like objects from school supply catalogs.

▶ Draw around different shapes of blocks, then label the block shelf with the shapes so children can match the shapes with blocks.

▶ Trace around art supplies (like scissors and glue bottles) or utensils in the housekeeping area (like pans and cups). Attach the outlines to the shelves with clear contact so children know where things belong.

 CLEAN-UP TOOLS

Shaving Cream Clean-Up

When?

Finger painting with shaving cream cleans tables and hands and makes the room smell good, too!

Why?

This is a wonderful sensory activity that encourages children to clean up together.

What?

can of shaving cream
paper towels
sponges and water

How?

➤ Squirt a small (very small!) pile of shaving cream onto a table, shelf or cabinet that needs to be cleaned.

➤ Let the children finger paint with it and enjoy the experience.

➤ When they are finished, give them paper towels to wipe up the excess, then clean with a wet sponge.

Adaptations

➤ On the playground, finger paint with shaving cream on low windows, then hose off.

➤ Add a drop of food coloring to the shaving cream, or experiment with different brands or scents.

▶▶▶▶▶▶▶ 5 ▶▶▶▶▶▶▶

ATTENTION GETTERS

Throughout the day, you will need to get children's attention to change activities and give directions. Rather than raising your voice or giving direct commands, blink the lights, tell the children to "freeze" or try one of the fun activities in this chapter. It's important to use a wide variety of techniques to focus children's attention and keep the classroom full of surprises. You never know what's going to work with a particular group of children, so experiment, adapt and invent a few new techniques of your own. Keep the tone positive, and the children will be entertained and will gladly follow along.

SONGS

Pretty Butterfly

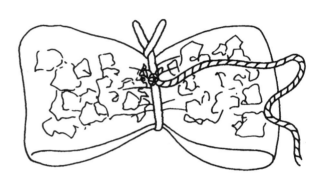

When?

Pretty Butterfly sparks children's interest and gets their hands in their lap in a positive way.

Why?

When children are singing and doing motions to a song, they're not poking others or disrupting the group.

What?

No materials are needed.

How?

▶ Clasp thumbs together and flutter fingers around like a butterfly while singing the following song to the tune of "Twinkle, Twinkle, Little Star."

▶ Let the children watch at first, then follow along.

Pretty, pretty butterfly (flutter hands like a butterfly)
Flying up in the sky.
Pretty, pretty butterfly,
Fly, fly, fly, fly.
Light upon my shoulder, (place butterfly on shoulders, then nose)
Then upon my nose.

Light upon my tummy, (place butterfly on tummy, then toes)
Then upon my toes.
Pretty, pretty butterfly (flutter hands, then place on head)
Light upon my head.
Pretty, pretty butterfly (put hands in lap)
Go to bed.

▶ Now that you have the children's attention, lower your voice and talk softly so you don't wake the butterflies.

Adaptation

▶ Let the children make a butterfly to use as they sing this song. Give each child a sandwich baggie, some tissue paper and a pipe cleaner. Let him tear up the tissue paper and put it in the baggie. Tuck in the end of the plastic bag, then wrap the pipe cleaner around it to make a body and antennae. Attach a piece of yarn for flying.

 SONGS

Follow Me

When?

Sing this song to calm children and focus their attention.

Why?

This activity challenges children to join along by carefully listening and following the actions.

What?

No materials are needed.

How?

► Do the motions while singing the following to the tune of "Shortnin' Bread."

Everybody do this, do this, do this. (clap hands)
Everybody do this and follow me.

Touch your shoulders, shoulders, shoulders.
Touch your shoulders and follow me. (touch shoulders)

► Continue singing this song with different motions such as jumping jacks, toe touches, move arms in circles, etc.

► Make the motions simple or more complex depending on the abilities of the children.

► For the last verse, sing, "Everybody line up," "Everybody listen," or whatever transition is necessary.

Adaptations

► Change the words of the song to help children sit down quietly.

Everybody have a seat, have a seat, have a seat.
Everybody have a seat on the floor.
Not on the ceiling, not on the door.
Everybody have a seat on the floor.

► Teach opposites by singing the following song and doing the motions.

Top and bottom, top and bottom, (touch top of head, then bottoms of feet)
Top and bottom and give a little clap.
Top and bottom, top and bottom,
Top and bottom and put them in your lap.
Front and back...(clap in front, then behind)
Loud and soft...(sing "loud", then "soft")
High and low...(clap up, then clap down low)
Over and under...(clap over head, then under knees)
Beside and between...(put hands by side, then between legs)

▶▶▶▶▶▶ SONGS ▶▶▶▶▶▶

Band Conductor

When?

Use this technique when moving children from a noisy activity to a quiet one.

Why?

Following the band conductor helps children follow directions and become aware of the difference between loud and soft sounds.

What?

No materials are needed.

How?

▶ After singing a song with a normal voice, tell the children that they're going to be the band and that you'll be their conductor.

▶ When you stretch your arms out wide they can sing loud, but when you bring your hands together in front of you they should use a very soft voice.

▶ Practice having them vary their voices from loud to soft with a single note, then try it with some familiar songs like "The Alphabet Song," "The Wheels on the Bus" or "The Eensy Weensy Spider."

▶ End the song with your hands together in front of you.

▶ Speak to the children in a whisper voice.

Adaptations

▶ Sing songs with "silly voices" that will also reinforce different musical concepts such as:

Rabbit voice—fast
Turtle voice—slow
Monster voice—big and deep
Mouse voice—high and soft

▶ Let children take turns being the conductor as their friends follow along.

▶▶▶▶▶▶   FINGER PLAYS   ▶▶▶▶▶▶

The Finger Band

When?

The Finger Band calms children down after active play, preparing them for a story or quiet time.

Why?

Finger plays develop verbal skills, auditory memory and small motor skills.

What?

No materials are needed.

How?

▶ Recite the finger play, making the appropriate motions.

The finger band is coming to town, (put hands behind back, then wiggle them as you bring them out in front of you)
Coming to town, coming to town.
The finger band is coming to town,
So early in the morning.
This is the way we play our drums, (pretend to play drums with your hands)
Play our drums, play our drums.
This is the way we play our drums,
So early in the morning.
This is the way we play our horns... (pretend to blow horns)
This is the way we twirl our hats... (pretend to twirl hats)

▶ Ask children to suggest other instruments that could be in the band and make the appropriate motions.

▶ End with the verse below.

The finger band is going away, (march hands behind your back as you lower your voice)
Going away, going away.
The finger band is going away,
So early in the morning.

▶ By the time you get to the last line, your voice should be a whisper, and the children should be settled down and looking at you quietly.

Adaptation

▶ Sing The Finger Band to the tune of "The Mulberry Bush."

 FINGER PLAYS

Two Little Blackbirds

1. 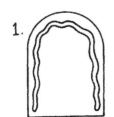 2. 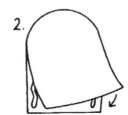 3.  4.

When?

Pull two little blackbirds out of a pocket to get children's attention any time during the day.

Why?

Children enjoy these little finger puppets because they are something to focus on and follow along with the motions.

Body
Cut 4

black felt

Wings
Cut 4

black felt

Beaks
Cut 2
yellow felt

What?

black felt (9" x 12")
yellow felt scraps
glue gun or fabric glue
4 wiggly eyes
scissors

Preparation

▶ Trace and cut around the patterns.

▶ Glue around the curved edges of the two body pieces and press together to make a finger puppet. Glue on the eyes and beak. Glue the wings to the back of the body.

How?

▶ Put one puppet on each forefinger, and hide them behind your back.

▶ Pull out one at a time, sit it on your shoulder and say the following.

Two little blackbirds (put puppets on shoulders)
Sitting on a hill.
One named Jack, (wiggle puppet on right)
And the other named Jill. (wiggle puppet on left)
Fly away, Jack. (fly right behind you)
Fly away, Jill. (fly left behind you)
Come back, Jack. (bring back right)
Come back, Jill. (bring back left)
Two little blackbirds
Sitting on a hill.

Adaptations

▶ To quiet the children, just mouth the words to the poem and do the motions.

▶ Let two children pretend to be the blackbirds and act out the motions.

▶ Make other animals and characters for songs and stories.

▶▶▶▶▶▶▶ FINGER PLAYS ▶▶▶▶▶▶▶

Make a Lap

When?

This little poem helps children sit down or stand up.

Why?

When children repeat the words and make the motions, they settle down.

What?

No materials are needed.

How?

▶ Ask the children to repeat each line.

▶ Model the motions for the children.

I tap my head.
I push my nose.
I pull my ear.
I touch my toes.
I clap, clap, clap.
Then I sit down
And make my lap.

Adaptations

▶ If children are sitting, say this verse to get them to stand up.

I tap my head.
I push my nose.
I pull my ear.
I touch my toes.
I clap, clap, clap.
Then I stand up.
Uh, oh, where's my lap?

▶ Sing this song to the tune of "If you're Happy and You Know It," to encourage children to sit down.

Put your bottom on the rug,
*   on the rug,*
Put your bottom on the rug,
*   on the rug,*
Put your bottom on the rug,
*   then give yourself a hug,*
Put your bottom on the rug,
*   on the rug.*

▶▶▶▶▶▶ FINGER PLAYS ▶▶▶▶▶▶

Mr. Smith and Mr. Brown

When?

This finger play settles restless children.

Why?

Children practice speaking and sequencing skills as they tell the story of "Mr. Smith and Mr. Brown."

What?

No materials are needed.

How?

▶ Open hands, put in thumbs, close fingers over thumbs to make a fist, then begin the finger play.

> One day Mr. Smith opened his door, (open right fist)
> Went outside, closed his door, (wiggle right thumb, close fingers)
> And said, "What a beautiful day.
> I'm going to go visit Mr. Brown."
> So Mr. Smith went up the hill, (move right thumb up and down in front of you)
> And down the hill,
> And up the hill,
> And down the hill.
> When he got to Mr. Brown's house
> He knocked on the door and said, (knock on left fist)
> "Oh, Mr. Brown, Oh, Mr. Brown."

> Nobody answered, so he went and
> Knocked on the back door. (knock on back of left fist)
> "Oh, Mr. Brown, Oh, Mr. Brown.
> I guess he's not at home."
> So Mr. Smith went up the hill, (move right thumb up and down in front of you)
> And down the hill,
> And up the hill,
> And down the hill.
> And when he got home, he opened (open fingers and stick thumb inside)
> His door, went inside,
> And closed his door.

> The next day Mr. Brown opened his door...(continue doing the finger play using the opposite hand as Mr. Brown)

> On the third day Mr. Smith and Mr. Brown both opened their doors... (Continue the finger play as before with both of them. Have them meet each other and dance around and play together.
> Then they both go home, open their doors, close their doors and go to sleep. Put hands together and rest head.)

Adaptation

▶ Change the names of the characters by using the names of children in the class, storybook characters (Baby Bear and Goldilocks) or seasonal figures (Frosty and Santa).

▶▶▶▶▶▶ FINGER PLAYS ▶▶▶▶▶▶▶

Wiggle Them

When?

Wiggle Them gets the wiggles out of children so they can pay attention.

Why?

Finger plays contribute to language development and keep little hands busy in a constructive way.

What?

No materials are needed.

How?

▶ Begin saying the poem and doing the motions. The children will naturally join in.

Wiggle them, wiggle them, (wiggle fingers in front of you)
Wiggle them so.
Wiggle them high, (wiggle over head)
And wiggle them low. (wiggle near floor)
Wiggle to the left. (wiggle to left)
Wiggle to the right. (wiggle to right)
Wiggle them, wiggle them, (wiggle behind your back)
Out of sight.
Clap them... (clap hands)
Roll them... (roll hands around)
Snap them... (snap fingers)

▶ End with an "opera clap," just tapping index fingers lightly together.

Adaptation

▶ Try singing this familiar finger play to the tune of "Shortnin' Bread".

Open them, shut them.
Open them, shut them.
Give a little, tiny clap.
Open them, shut them.
Open them, shut them.
Put them in your tiny lap.

 **FINGER PLAYS**

The Snap Rap

When?

This snappy rap focuses children's attention on the playground or in the classroom.

Why?

As children join in with the steady beat, they are encouraged to listen and follow directions.

What?

No materials are needed.

How?

► Simply start snapping your fingers.

► When the children are looking and snapping along, say the following chant.

If you want to hear a story, (snap to the beat)
This is what you do.
You've got to sit down on the rug
Like the soldiers do.
You've got to listen to your teacher,
Raise your hand.
You've got to let her know
That you understand.
That's right, (snap and point to children
  following directions)
That's right.
That's right.
That's right.

Adaptations

► For children who can't snap, simply clap to the beat.

► Change the words to what the children are expected to do. For example, "If you want to go outside, this is what you do. You've got to line up at the door like the soldiers do."

► Do the Magic Clap. Tell the children that whenever you clap a pattern, they should stop, repeat it and look at you. Practice a few times, then give it a try on the playground or in the classroom when you need their attention.

 **FINGER PLAYS**

Little Mouse

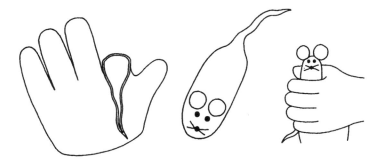

When?

Pull this little mouse out of a pocket to quiet children for stories or other activities.

Why?

Children will lower their voices so they don't scare the little mouse.

What?

old cloth glove
felt scraps
markers or paint pens
scissors
glue

Preparation

➤ Cut off the index finger of the glove to make the mouse's body and tail.

➤ Cut out ears from felt and glue them on.

➤ Draw on eyes, a nose and whiskers.

How?

➤ Stick an index finger in the mouse puppet, then hide it behind your back.

➤ In a soft voice, begin the finger play and slowly creep the mouse out from behind you.

A little mouse (hold up right index finger and wiggle)
Lived quietly in his hole.
A little mouse (make a hole with left hand and stick the right finger in it)
Lived quietly in his hole.
When all was as quiet,
As quiet as could be—
Sh! Sh! Sh!
Out popped he! (pull out right finger and wiggle)

Adaptation

➤ Make a bunny puppet or a caterpillar puppet from the other fingers of the glove.

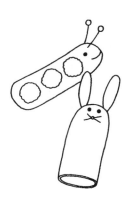

▶▶▶▶▶▶▶ QUIETING TRICKS ▶▶▶▶▶▶▶

Magic Wand

When?

Use the magic wand to calm children before story time, to prepare them to walk down the hall, to give directions, etc.

Why?

This idea works like magic to get children quiet and to encourage them to listen to directions.

What?

construction paper or poster board
stapler
scissors
glue
glitter
straw
gold or silver spray paint (optional)

Preparation

▶ Cut a star out of paper or poster board.

▶ Staple the star to the end of the straw to make a wand and spray paint it gold or silver if desired.

▶ Decorate star with glitter.

How?

▶ Take the magic wand and tell the children, "When I wave my wand over you, you'll feel the quiet magic and be ready for our story."

▶ Most children will pretend to feel the magic. For the child who doesn't play along, say, "You may hold the magic wand."

Adaptations

▶ Let one child hold the magic wand and gently tap quiet friends on the head to dismiss them.

▶ Have each child hold the wand and tell a special wish.

Rain Stick

When?

Relax and calm children for a quiet activity or rest with the rain stick.

Why?

Children will want to be quiet in order to hear the peaceful sound the rain stick makes.

What?

cardboard roller (from wrapping paper)
aluminum foil
masking tape
rice

Preparation

▶ Tape closed one end of the cardboard tube.

▶ Take a long sheet of aluminum foil and loosely roll it up lengthwise. It should be 1/2" to 3/4" thick.

▶ Bend the foil coil back and forth in a continuous "S" shape, then insert it into the open end of the tube.

▶ Continue bending the aluminum foil and sliding it into the tube until you reach the top. Do not pack it in too tightly.

▶ Add approximately 1/2 cup of rice to the tube. (The amount used will vary according to the size of the tube. Experiment with different amounts of rice to get the sound you like.)

▶ Tape up the other end of the tube, then decorate the outside with markers, if desired.

How?

▶ Pick up the rain stick and slowly rotate it to make the sound of rain.

▶ Ask the children to listen closely to see if they can hear it raining.

▶ As the children quiet down to listen to the peaceful sound of the rain stick, give the directions for a new activity, prepare the children for rest or any other transition.

Adaptations

▶ Purchase ready-made rain sticks at most nature stores.

▶ Vary the size of the cardboard tube and the objects in it. With a larger tube, try unpopped popcorn, macaroni and beans. For smaller tubes, salt and grits work well.

 QUIETING TRICKS

Glitter Bottles

When?

Use glitter bottles at circle time or at nap time to relax children.

Why?

Children have something to hold and play with so they keep their hands to themselves.

What?

small plastic bottles with lids
glitter
food coloring
water
optional, glue gun

Preparation

▶ Put one to two teaspoons of glitter in the bottom of the bottle.

▶ Fill to the top with water, then add a few drops of food coloring.

▶ Screw the top on securely. (Use a glue gun for added safety.)

How?

▶ As children join the circle, give them a bottle to hold and turn.

▶ When it is rest time, let children lie on their cots and have a bottle to look at.

Adaptations

▶ At nap time, tell children the bottles have "sleepy time dust" in them.

▶ Make an "ocean in a bottle" by filling a plastic container 2/3 with water. Add a few drops of food coloring, then fill it to the top with vegetable oil. Move the bottle slowly to make "waves."

▶ Bubble bottles can be made by filling a bottle halfway with water, then adding a squirt of detergent and a little food coloring. Glue on the top, then shake, shake, shake.

▶ Pour 1/2 cup of corn syrup in a plastic bottle, then add food coloring. Slowly move the bottle and watch the liquid coat the sides.

Squat and Sit

When?

Get children's attention with this game.

Why?

Many times children forget where they are, and this technique will bring them back to reality, help them regain self-control and focus on what they should be doing.

What?

No materials are needed.

How?

▶ If children are running around the room and are out of control, call out "Squat and Sit" and wait for them to squat down on the ground or sit on the floor.

▶ When the children are still, whisper what you want them to do, or go around the room and tap them on the head to signal they may get up and move again.

Adaptations

▶ On the playground or in the middle of a game, tell children to stop and put their hands on their heads.

▶ Call out "1-2-3 Freeze" and wait for the children to freeze in place. Then give them directions.

▶ Turn off the lights to calm children down.

▶ Change your voice to get children's attention. Make it high and squeaky, then low like a growl.

 QUIETING TRICKS

Follow the Flashlight

When?

Use a flashlight to change the pace in the room and gather children in a group.

Why?

As children follow along in this game, they are practicing visual tracking.

What?

flashlight

How?

➤ Turn off the lights.

➤ Tell the children to get behind you, and follow the trail the flashlight shines on the floor.

➤ When the children are ready, walk around the room making an imaginary trail on the floor with the flashlight.

➤ After walking around the room in a creative pattern, sit down quietly on the floor, turn off the flashlight and speak quietly to the children about what they will do next.

Adaptations

➤ To make different colors of light, cover the flashlight with colored cellophane held in place with a rubber band.

➤ Let the children hold the flashlight and shine a path for their friends to follow.

➤ Make designs on the ceiling with the flashlight.

➤ Let children make shadow animals on the wall with a flashlight or film projector.

Traffic Light

When?

The Traffic Light is a nonverbal way to communicate with children.

Why?

Children learn to monitor their behavior and develop self-control by responding to different signs and cues such as the Traffic Light.

What?

red, yellow, green and black construction paper
yarn or string
scissors
glue
hole punch

Preparation

▶ Cut out 8" circles from the red, yellow and green paper. Cut out three 8" black circles.

▶ Glue a black circle to each of the colored circles.

▶ Punch holes in the circles and tie them together like a traffic light with the yarn.

▶ Hang the traffic light on a wall in a prominent place in the room with the black circles showing.

How?

▶ Ask the children what the different colors on the traffic light mean.

▶ Explain that in the classroom the traffic light helps control noise.

▶ If the green light is showing, that means the noise is fine and the children can continue.

▶ When the yellow light is turned over, it means "caution" and the children need to lower their voices.

▶ If red appears, that means the children are too loud and must use a whisper voice.

▶ Control the noise level in the room with the traffic light by turning over different colors.

▶ Don't forget to change it to green when the children are quiet.

Adaptation

▶ Make other signs for the room such as "stop," "go" and "walk."

Finger Friends

When?

Surprise and entertain children with the help of a Finger Friend.

Why?

Children are fascinated with little characters and will want to hear what the Finger Friends have to say.

What?

fine tip washable markers

How?

▶ Draw some eyes, a nose and a mouth on an index finger before circle time (or any other transition time).

▶ Put your finger in your lap.

▶ When the children are sitting quietly say, "I brought a little friend to see you today."

▶ Hold up your finger and dance it in front of you.

▶ Let the children say hello to it, then sing a song or use it to introduce a new activity.

Adaptations

▶ Create different Finger Friends with bits of fabric, yarn and imagination.

▶ Draw a little puppet on each child's index finger, then use it to point to parts of the body or to follow simple directions such as "put it on your head," "hide it behind your back," etc.

▶ Use the Finger Friend to point to words on a language experience chart or big book.

▶ Start dancing your fingers on your head, shoulders and other parts of the body. As the children watch you, encourage them to follow along, then end by folding your hands quietly in front of you.

Pokey the Pony

When?

Have Pokey the Pony come to see the children before a story or when changing activities.

Why?

Shhh! They'll want to hear what Pokey has to say to them.

What?

old sock
needle and thread
yarn, button, two large wiggly eyes
red and black felt scraps
old cloth bag or pocket book

Preparation

► Put your hand in the sock and extend your thumb from your fingers. This will form the mouth for the pony.

► Sew on a button for the nose and two wiggly eyes.

► Cut a red mouth and two black ears from the felt scraps. The mouth should be an oval shape that fits into the sock "mouth" made by your thumb and fingers. Ears should be shaped like triangles.

► Sew on the mouth and ears, then sew on yarn for the mane.

► Put the pony in the bag, then cut a slit in the back so your hand can reach into the bag and manipulate the pony.

How?

► Before sitting down, put your hand in the hole and put on the puppet.

► Tell the children you have a new friend in the bag, but he's very shy and he'll only come out if they're very quiet.

► When the children are quiet, pop Pokey out of the bag and introduce him.

► Let Pokey whisper a riddle or give a clue about what your story or the next activity will be about.

► Make sure you put Pokey back on a high shelf after you're finished with him to keep his "magic" a secret.

Adaptation

► Put a book or prop in the bag which Pokey can pull out with his mouth.

▶▶▶▶▶▶ QUIETING TRICKS ▶▶▶▶▶▶

Special Spectacles

When?

Use these Special Spectacles to get children's attention anytime.

Why?

This is a positive cue that says, "I have something to tell you."

What?

No materials are needed.

How?

▶ Using thumb and index finger on both hands, form circles.

▶ Put these up next to your eyes to look like glasses as you say or sing the following.

I'm putting on my spectacles to see what I can see.
I'm putting on my spectacles and I see
(Child's name), and (child's name), and
(Child's name) looking at me.

▶ As the children quiet down, and make eye contact with you, say their names.

Adaptations

▶ Use empty glasses frames, or make some pretend glasses from pipe cleaners and plastic rings from a six pack drink holder.

▶ Encourage children to pretend to put on their "special spectacles" to look back at you.

▶ Have children put on "spectacles" before coming in from the playground to look at something they think is beautiful.

▶ Show children how to cup their hands behind their ears to make elephant ears so they can listen carefully to and remember directions.

▶ Use Special Spectacles for recall at the end of the day, For example, "Ishi, I saw you painting. Can you tell me about your picture?" "Erin, I saw you in blocks, what did you build?"

Teeny Tiny Friends

When?

Teeny Tiny Friends is another technique that helps focus children's attention.

Why?

These imaginary characters give children a reason to talk softly.

What?

old pocketbook, bag, school box, etc.
small toy figures (dolls, animals or anything children would be interested in)

How?

➤ Place the toys in the bag or box.

➤ Before the story, tell the children you have brought some little friends to visit with them, but the friends are very tiny and have teeny ears, so they will have to use tiny voices.

➤ When the children are quiet, carefully remove the toy figures from the box or pocketbook.

➤ If the children start to become too loud say, "Remember our little friends. Let's not hurt their little ears."

➤ When the story is over, have the children say good-bye to the tiny friends and return them to the bag or box.

Adaptations

➤ Tiny friends might come out at nap time and rest with children, or they might visit other activities in your room.

➤ Have children make up names for the friends and tell imaginary stories about them.

 QUIETING TRICKS

Make Rain

When?

The sound of rain brings peace to the classroom and calms children.

Why?

Children are enchanted by making the sound of rain which calms them down and enables them to follow directions.

What?

No materials are needed.

How?

➤ Ask the children to help make rain.

➤ Tell them they just need to watch you and do what you do.

➤ Make each of the sounds below for five or ten seconds.

Slide palms back and forth.
Tap fingers together.
Snap fingers.
Clap hands.
Slap thighs.
Stomp feet.
Slap thighs.
Clap hands.
Snap fingers.
Tap fingers together.
Slide your palms back and forth.
Lay your hands quietly in your lap.

Adaptation

➤ Make rain in a round. Divide the class into two groups. Have one side begin a motion, then bring in the other side a few seconds later. Continue working through all the motions. This works well if there is an adult to lead each group.

Give Me Five

When?

Give Me Five focuses children's attention.

Why?

This is a positive way to remind children to listen with their whole body.

What?

No materials are needed.

How?

► Tell the children that the class has a secret code that's just for you and them.

► When you say, "Give me five," and hold up your hand, they check the following five things, then return the "five" by holding up their hand.

- Eyes on the teacher.
- Ears listening.
- Mouth quiet.
- Arms by your side.
- Feet still.

Adaptations

► Make up other secret signs for the class such as two fingers in the air means to be as quiet as a bunny.

► Blow a train whistle, siren whistle, bird whistle or other type of whistle to get children's attention.

► Use different whistles for various commands. For example, a train whistle could mean get in line, or the bird whistle could mean clean-up.

▶▶▶▶▶▶ QUIETING TRICKS ▶▶▶▶▶▶▶

Cluck-Cluck Cup

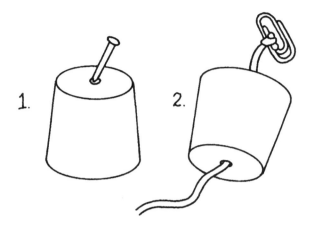
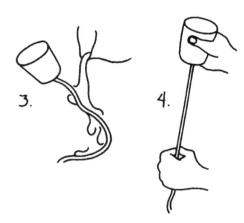

When?

The children's curiosity about this "clucking cup" will help you gather them for a group activity.

Why?

As children try to discover how the strange sound is made, they will be exercising scientific methods!

What?

plastic cup
18" string
scissors
paper clip
water

Preparation

▶ Poke a hole in the bottom of the cup with the point of the scissors or a nail.

▶ Thread the string through the hole and tie the paper clip to the end of the string in the cup.

How?

▶ Wet the string, hold the cup in one hand and tightly pull down on the string with the other hand.

▶ The string should make a squeaky, clucking sound. (Use more water and pull in jerky movements if it doesn't work.)

▶ As children come over to see what the noise is, ask them open-ended questions about what is making the sound.

Adaptation

▶ Try making other unusual sounds to get children's attention, or use musical instruments or a music box.

Nutkin

When?

Nutkin helps quiet children for a story or other activity.

Why?

Children's auditory discrimination skills are strengthened as they listen for Nutkin.

What?

potato chip canister or similar can with a lid
brown and gray construction paper
assorted nuts
popsicle stick
scissors
markers
tape

Preparation

► Cover the can with brown paper to resemble a tree trunk.

► Put a handful of nuts in the bottom of the can.

► Draw and cut a squirrel from the gray construction paper and tape it to the end of the popsicle stick.

► Place the squirrel puppet in the can with the nuts and put on the lid.

How?

► As the children sit down for circle or story, take the can and say, "I wonder if Nutkin is at home. If you're quiet maybe you can hear him rattling his nuts."

► Shake the can.

► When all the children are focused, quietly pull the little squirrel puppet out and let it introduce a new activity or tell the children a story.

Adaptations

► Hide nuts on the playground, and let the children try and find them like squirrels.

► Count and sort the nuts in the can, or use them for other math activities.

 QUIETING TRICKS

Bubble Machine

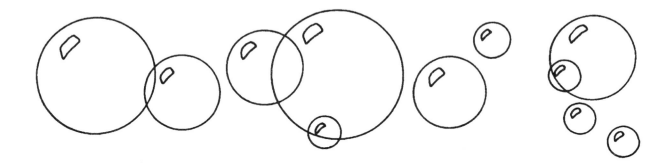

When?

Use the Bubble Machine to gather children for a group activity.

Why?

Children are fascinated when they see the bubbles and will want to join you.

What?

margarine tub
straw
bottle of bubbles (Purchase one or make your own.)
hole punch

Preparation

▶ Punch two holes in the lid of the margarine tub.

▶ Pour about 1/2 cup of the bubble solution in the tub.

▶ Put the top back on. Insert the straw in one of the holes and blow until bubbles come out the other hole.

How?

▶ Demonstrate how the Bubble Machine works.

▶ Tell the children that whenever they see it they should come sit down on the rug.

▶ Challenge the children to sit down before all the bubbles pop.

Adaptation

▶ Just blow bubbles with the wand in the bubble solution to get children's attention.

LINE-UP

Moving children smoothly from one area of the room or building to another or from indoors to outside can be a challenge. Although you don't want to sound like a drill sergeant with children lined up like little soldiers behind you, you do need to have some routine and organization. It is developmentally appropriate to allow younger children to move in small groups or with a buddy.

When lining up, it is easier on everyone if you add an imaginative element of fun. Pretend to be butterflies, or move quietly like snow; tiptoe like mice, or glide silently as clouds. Another helpful management technique, if there are two teachers in the room, is to divide children into smaller groups. One teacher can go outside with those who are ready, while the other teacher can assist the others. This saves children from waiting and becoming restless, while giving more individual help to children who might need it.

 MOVING RIGHT ALONG

Spaghetti, Grapes, Pumpkins and Oranges

When?

Use this technique when it's time to line up or organize the children in the room or on the playground.

Why?

A potentially difficult transition is both fun and interesting when approached as a game. The suggestions below also encourage children to listen and follow directions.

What?

No materials are needed.

How?

▶ Tell the children that when they hear certain words, they are to do the following actions.

Spaghetti—Children line up in single file and place their right hand on the shoulder of the person in front of them.

Oranges—Children hold hands and stand in a circle.

Grapes—Children cluster around you like grapes.

Pumpkins—Children sit cross-legged on the ground like pumpkins in a pumpkin patch.

Adaptations

▶ With young children, use one word at a time. Change it every few weeks.

▶ Have children pretend to get in their cars, boats, planes or other vehicles and drive or fly to other places in the building.

 MOVING RIGHT ALONG

Line-Up Rap

When?

Use this rap to line up before going down halls or moving to another area of the school.

Why?

Children enjoy lining up while being reminded of appropriate behavior.

What?

No materials are needed.

How?

▶ Snap fingers or clap hands and start the following rap.

Every line has a leader
And it has a caboose,
So keep your line straight,
And not too loose.
Walk and walk
And walk in line.
Keep your hands to yourself
And you'll do just fine.

Adaptation

▶ Before leaving the room ask, "Who can remind us how we should walk in the hall?" Let the children remind each other of appropriate behavior. Remember, rules and expectations need to be reinforced and children need to be reminded frequently.

Sign Language

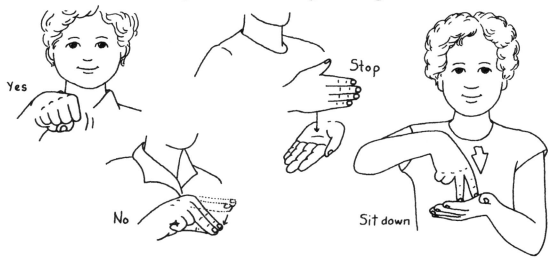

When?

Give the children directions for lining up and other commands with sign language.

Why?

This helps children understand how people with hearing difficulties communicate with each other, and it will lower the noise level in the room.

What?

No materials are needed.

How?

► Introduce sign language by asking children if they know someone who cannot hear.

► Explain that when people can't hear, they use their hands to communicate with each other. This is called sign language.

► Demonstrate one or two of the commands shown, then let the children do them with you.

► When telling the children what to do, challenge them to look at you and follow the sign.

Adaptations

► As children master one or two signs, add more to their repertoire.

► Give each child in the room a sign language name. When dismissing the children from the group, tell them to watch carefully and they may leave when you make their sign.

► Introduce children to the sign language alphabet. Practice doing the different letters.

 MOVING RIGHT ALONG

Silly Snake

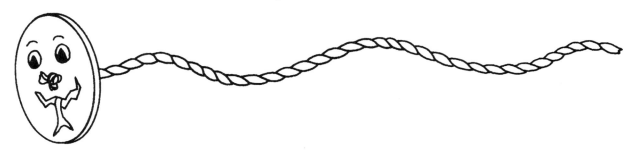

When?

A Silly Snake to hold on to provides a safe way to move little ones or children with special needs.

Why?

This idea helps keep children focused so they don't wander away from the group.

What?

12' piece of rope
lid from a plastic container
markers
scissors

Preparation

- ▶ Poke a hole in the middle of the lid with scissors. Push the end of the rope through the hole and tie a knot.

- ▶ Decorate the lid with markers to look like a silly snake face.

How?

- ▶ Choose a leader to hold on to the rope at the snake's head.

- ▶ Let the other children grab on to the rope.

- ▶ Tell them to hold the snake tightly so it doesn't get away.

- ▶ Lead them outside.

Adaptations

- ▶ Tie plastic bracelets or other small toys onto a rope for children to hold as they walk.

- ▶ Let children make little ponies to ride to the playground. To make the pony's head, decorate a paper lunch sack and stuff it with strips of newspaper. Tightly roll up three sheets of newspaper lengthwise and tape it to make a stick for the pony. Put the sack head on one end of the stick and tape it in place. Giddy-up!

- ▶ Lay the Silly Snake on the ground and jump over it or walk on it like a balance beam.

- ▶ Make shapes and letters on the floor with Silly Snake.

 MOVING RIGHT ALONG

Listen–Up—Line–Up

When?

Line up or move to another activity with this listening game.

Why?

Instead of running and rushing, children learn to listen and follow directions.

What?

No materials are needed.

How?

▶ Ask children to listen carefully.

▶ When they hear the color of clothing they have on, they may line up. "Everyone with yellow may line up. Everyone wearing purple, etc."

Adaptations

▶ Call out different types of shoes, like buckle shoes, Velcro shoes, white tie shoes, etc.

▶ If children know the month in which they were born, call out different months of the year. They line up when they hear their birth month.

▶ Take a picture of each child and put a small piece of felt or Velcro on the back. Tell the children to watch and when you put their picture up on the flannel board they may be excused.

▶ Make up a little rhyme for each child. For example, "I know a little girl named Sarah. She stands up, turns around and hops to the table." "I know a little boy named Paulo. He likes to stand up, jump up and down, then skip to the table."

 MOVING RIGHT ALONG

Outside Voices

When?

This idea helps children differentiate between loud and soft voices when they come indoors.

Why?

Often children forget where they are and need to be reminded about behavior that is appropriate for different places. This routine will be a positive reminder about the transition from outdoors to indoors.

What?

lunch sack or other decorative bag

How?

► Have a class discussion about the difference between the loud voices that are used on the playground and the quiet voices used inside.

► Demonstrate outside and inside voices.

► Explain why softer voices are needed inside.

► Show the children the bag.

► Tell them that when they come in from play time, they can put their outside voices in the bag so they won't hurt anyone's ears or disturb others.

► Hang the bag by the door, and let the children put their loud voices in it as they come into the room.

Adaptation

► Choose a child to hold the bag and collect the outside voices.

 MOVING RIGHT ALONG

Number Please

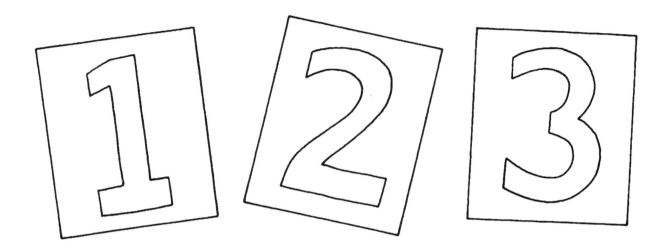

When?

This idea turns getting in line into a game.

Why?

Number Please reinforces numerical order while streamlining the lining up process.

What?

poster board or heavy paper
scissors
markers

Preparation

➤ Cut the poster board into 3" squares. You will need one for each child.

➤ Print a numeral on each card.

How?

➤ Before asking children to line up, give each child a card.

➤ Ask, "Who has 1?" That child gets in line followed by 2, 3, 4, etc.

➤ Let the first child collect the cards before moving to the next activity.

Adaptations

➤ Change the shape of the cards for different seasons or themes such as fish, dinosaurs, train cars, butterflies or valentines.

➤ Have children count in Spanish, Chinese or other languages as they line up.

Funny Feet

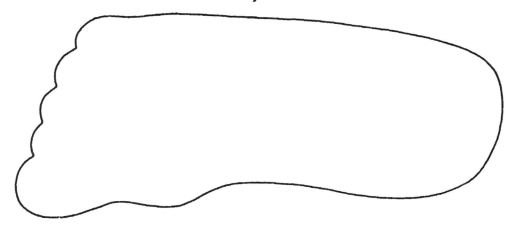

When?

Funny Feet on the floor prevent pushing and shoving as children line up.

Why?

Children have a designated place to stand and something to do.

What?

construction paper (different colors)
scissors
clear contact

Preparation

► Cut pairs of footprints out of colored construction paper.

► Line the footprints up on the floor in funny positions.

► Cover with clear contact.

How?

► Tell the children to find a pair of Funny Feet to stand on when it's time to line up.

Adaptations

► When dismissing children from circle, ask them to stand on red feet, blue feet, etc.

► Place Funny Feet on the floor by centers to designate how many children can play there. For example, put two pairs of feet at the easel, four pairs by blocks, etc.

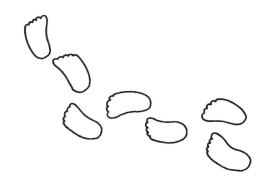

 DISMISSAL

Echo

When?

Dismiss children to centers, to line up or to another activity with the echo game.

Why?

This game develops listening skills and auditory memory.

What?

No materials are needed.

How?

► Ask children if they know what an echo is.

► Explain that an echo repeats a noise or what a person says.

► That's what they get to do in the echo game.

> *Teacher says: "Yoo hoo!"*
> *Children repeat: "Yoo hoo!"*
> *Teacher says: "Do what I do."*
> *Children repeat: "Do what I do."*
> *Teacher claps three times.*
> *Children clap three times.*

► Continue slapping, clapping and snapping out different beats and rhythms with the children responding to each one.

► Give each child an opportunity to repeat a pattern.

► Each child is dismissed after he's had a turn.

Adaptations

► Let children take turns being leaders in this game as the other children echo what they say or do.

► Play the mirror game and have children mimic your actions.

► Use a toy drum, xylophone or other instrument and let the children repeat what you play on it.

 DISMISSAL

What If?

When?

Play What If to dismiss children from circle or whenever there are a few extra minutes.

Why?

Problem-solving, creativity and language skills are reinforced with this open-ended activity. It is also an effective tool for understanding children and some of their inner feelings.

What?

No materials are needed.

How?

► Begin by saying, "Let's play a pretend game. What if you were an animal? What kind of animal would you be? Why?"

► One at a time let the children tell you what kind of animal they would be and move like that animal to a center (or to snack, etc.).

► As there is no right or wrong response to What If questions, children are encouraged to think creatively.

Adaptations

► What if you found a magic lamp? What would you wish for?

► What if you had a magic carpet? Where would you go?

► What if you could have a birthday and be any age you wanted to be? How old would you be? Why?

► What if you were the teacher? What would you do?

► What if you were a giant dinosaur? What would you do?

► What if you were green? What would you be?

► What if you found $100?

► What if you got lost in a big store?

► What if you could trade places with someone? Who would you be?

► What if you were grown-up? What would you do?

 DISMISSAL

Center Cards

When?

Use Center Cards when dismissing children from circle to centers or other activities.

Why?

Center Cards help children follow directions and give them an opportunity to experience an area of the room they might not choose on their own.

What?

school supply catalog
poster board cut into 4" x 6" rectangles
scissors
glue

Preparation

➤ Draw or cut out pictures representing various centers or activities. Make the number of pictures for each center match the number of children who can play in that area. For example, cut out two pictures of a sand or water table, four of blocks, two for easel painting, etc.

➤ Glue the pictures to the poster board.

How?

➤ Mix up the cards and turn them over so the pictures face down.

➤ Let one child at a time come up and choose a card.

➤ Although children are usually allowed to make their own choices, use Center Cards occasionally to provide variety.

Adaptation

➤ Play "show me" with the Center Cards. Have children match up the pictures on the cards with real objects in the classroom.

▶▶▶▶▶▶▶   DISMISSAL   ▶▶▶▶▶▶▶

Invisible Writing

When?

Write invisible shapes, letters or numerals on children's backs to dismiss them individually to another activity.

Why?

This game improves sensory perception while reinforcing concepts such as shapes.

What?

No materials are needed.

How?

▶ Move behind a child.

▶ Tell her you are going to draw a shape on her back.

▶ After she has identified the shape, she can move along.

▶ Draw the shape again if she has difficulty.

Adaptations

▶ For older children, draw letters or numerals on their backs.

▶ For younger children, draw letters or shapes on their hands.

▶ Divide children into pairs. Let them play a guessing game by drawing shapes, letters or numerals on each other's backs.

DISMISSAL

Pick a Pair

When?

Children find a friend to line up or play with when they Pick a Pair.

Why?

Visual discrimination and friendships are enhanced by this game.

What?

poster board
scissors
stickers or matching pictures
glue

Preparation

▶ Cut the poster board into 4" x 6" rectangles. You will need one for each child.

▶ Glue similar pictures or stickers on two cards so that you have pairs of matching cards.

How?

▶ Shuffle the cards.

▶ Let each child choose one.

▶ Tell the children to find the person who has the matching card.

▶ When they find their partner, they can both line up, go to a center, sit down at the table for lunch, etc.

Adaptations

▶ Depending on the developmental level of the children, draw pairs of shapes, sets and matching numerals and other matching information on the cards.

▶ Play a concentration game with the cards.

▶ Get paint chip strips from the paint store, two of each strip. Cut them apart, then let children match up like colors.

▶▶▶▶▶▶▶   DISMISSAL   ▶▶▶▶▶▶▶

Phone Fun

When?

The telephone is a handy toy for planning daily activities and moving children to activities.

Why?

This idea gives children the opportunity to think about what they want to do, then follow through with their plans.

What?

play telephone
bell

How?

▶ Hold the phone in your lap, then ring the bell.

▶ Call a child's name and tell him the phone call is for him.

▶ When the child answers the phone ask him, "Where would you like to play at school today?" or "What would you like to do today?"

▶ After the child has told you his plans, he can hang up the phone and move to that area of the room.

▶ Continue ringing the bell and calling other children forward to tell their plans for the day.

Adaptations

▶ Use a real telephone that doesn't work anymore.

▶ Purchase a play cellular phone. Ring it to get children's attention or pass it around and let children talk in it.

▶ Tie a piece of string or yarn between two paper cups to make a play telephone.

▶ Let the children dictate what they want to do on a language experience chart, then use it as a follow-up activity to review what they did or learned.

▶ Hold a stuffed animal or puppet in your lap. Have the children come up one at a time and tell it what they would like to do.

▶ Pass the phone around at the end of the day and let children tell what they enjoyed most or learned that day.

Choice Board

Blocks ⬜▭	Dramatic Play
Art 🖌	Library 📖
Manipulatives	Music ♩ ♩ ♫
Science 🍂	Water 🥣

When?

Let children use this board to choose a center or activity they would like to do.

Why?

This activity encourages children to make choices, and the teacher is able to assure appropriate group sizes for each activity.

What?

poster board
clothespins (spring type)
markers
school supply catalogs
scissors
glue

Preparation

▶ Decide what centers are available.

▶ Divide the poster board into different sections, write the name of each center in a section, then cut picture clues from the school supply catalog and glue them next to the appropriate word.

▶ Put a number of dots by each center, near the edge of the poster board, to represent how many children can play there. Be sure to have at least enough places to accommodate everyone, with a few extra spots.

▶ Write each child's name on a clothespin.

How?

► Pass out the clothespins to the children.

► Let them come up and clip their clothespin on a dot for the center where they would like to play.

► When they are tired of playing in the area, they move their clothespin to another center which has an available space.

Adaptations

► Make paper necklaces for the number of children who can play in each center. These could be color coded to the color of the sign labeling that center. For example, orange circle necklaces for housekeeping, etc. Children wear a necklace while they play in each center, then take it off when they want to leave.

► Glue two or four library pockets (or envelopes cut in half) to each center sign. Give each child an index card with her name printed at the top. When the children want to play in a particular area, they put their cards in a pocket.

 DISMISSAL

This Is the Way I Put on My Coat

When?

Sing this song as children put on hats and coats to go outside.

Why?

This common routine moves much more smoothly if children are singing a song and concentrating on what they are doing.

What?

hats
coats
mittens, boots, etc.

How?

► Sing the following to the tune of "Mulberry Bush."

► Model the motions for the children.

This is the way I put on my coat,
Put on my coat, put on my coat.
This is the way I put on my coat
Before I go out to play.

► Add verses for other pieces of clothing such as boots, hats, mittens, etc.

Adaptations

► Here's a trick to help little ones get their coats on. Have the child put his coat on the floor, then walk around it so he's standing next to the collar. Show him how to put his hands in the arms, then flip the coat over his head. He'll be dressed in a snap!

► To help children get shoes on the right feet, line the shoes up in pairs. Put a small dot with a marker on the inside of each shoe so the dots line up. All the children have to do is match the dots and their shoes will be on the correct feet.

▶▶▶▶▶▶▶ 7 ▶▶▶▶▶▶▶

LET'S EAT & NAP TIME

Eating snacks or meals together should be a pleasant, relaxed time when you and the children can enjoy each other's company and have informal conversations. It is important for teachers to sit down and eat family-style with children, modeling good manners and eating habits.

Make use of "teachable moments" to show children how to ask for food to be passed and other table courtesies. If children spill during the meal, calmly ask them to clean it up or offer to help them. When children are through eating, encourage them to sit at the table and visit, or excuse them to look at books or another quiet activity.

To make mealtime special, play music, turn off the lights, have a candlelight lunch (battery candles) or put flowers on the table. Relate meals to classroom themes, or plan special menus for holidays and other celebrations.

Another transition discussed in this chapter is nap time. Certainly the attitude you have about rest and the consistency you provide will influence the children. After lunch, begin talking about how good it's going to feel to rest. Encourage children to help you get out mats or cots as you turn off the lights and begin to wind down. Quietly singing

and humming lullabies can be very calming. It is very important to follow the same routine every day so children learn not only what to expect, but what behavior is expected of them. Here's a simple schedule that will prepare children for nap time.

▶ As children finish lunch, turn off the lights, close the curtains and softly play or sing appropriate music. (This is a good time to expose children to classical music.)

▶ Children should use the bathroom, wash their hands and brush their teeth.

▶ Children choose a book, get their sleepy time friend (animal or blanket) and lie on their cots.

▶ As children settle down, the teacher goes around, collects their books and "tucks them in" with a hug or back rub.

Scrub and Rub

When?

Getting children to wash their hands properly is a snap with this song.

Why?

Hand washing is a critical health habit that children should automatically do before eating or after toileting. Indeed, many diseases and germs can be eliminated with proper hand washing.

What?

No materials are needed.

How?

► Discuss with the children why it is important for them to wash their hands, then demonstrate properly how they should do it.

► Hands should be rinsed with the fingers slanted down, scrubbed vigorously for ten seconds, rinsed and dried with a paper towel.

► The faucet should then be turned off with the paper towel and the towel thrown away.

► Teach the children to sing the following song while they are scrubbing their hands with soap. Encourage them to make bubbles as they scrub.

► Sing the song to the tune of "Row, Row, Row Your Boat."

Wash, wash, wash your hands,
Play the handy game.
Scrub and rub and rub and scrub,
Germs go down the drain.

Adaptation

► Make a rebus sign to post by the sink which illustrates the steps for hand washing.

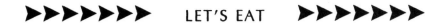
LET'S EAT

A Little Lotion

When?

Here's another technique to encourage children to wash their hands.

Why?

Smelling lotion and rubbing it into hands provides sensory stimulation and turns an ordinary routine into something children enjoy.

What?

hand lotion (non-allergenic)

How?

➤ After the children have washed their hands for snack or lunch, give them a little (very little!) hand lotion.

➤ Then they sit down and rub it on their hands as they wait for the other children.

Adaptations

➤ Demonstrate how to massage fingers and hands with the lotion.

➤ Put a lotion dispenser near the sink for children to use after other hand washing times.

 LET'S EAT

Set the Table

When?

Help children set the table for snack or lunch with this matching game.

Why?

This activity enhances one-to-one correspondence and other math skills.

What?

construction paper
scissors
markers
clear contact

Preparation

▶ Cut placemats from construction paper to fit the table.

▶ Draw the outline of cups, plates, napkins and utensils on the placemats.

▶ Cover with clear contact or laminate.

How?

▶ Table helpers put the placemats out, then set the table matching up the items using one-to-one correspondence.

▶ And don't forget to have one chair at each place!

Adaptations

▶ Use wallpaper, wrapping paper or contact paper to make the placemats. Cut them into oval shapes or scallop the edges.

▶ Let the children decorate their own placemats, adding their names if desired.

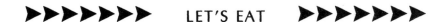

Name Hunt

When?

This transition technique helps children sit down quietly for snack or lunch.

Why?

Children learn to recognize their names, and since seating is random, they will be exposed to different friends.

What?

sentence strips, index cards or tagboard cut into 8" x 4" pieces
markers
basket
clear contact

Preparation

▶ Print each child's name on a strip of paper.

▶ Laminate the name cards or cover with clear contact.

How?

▶ Place the name cards in a basket, then let one child place a name by each seat. (This could be the person who is setting the table or a separate helper.)

▶ As the children come to the table, they find their names and then sit down at that place.

▶ After the meal, choose a child to pick up the name cards and put them back in the basket.

Adaptations

▶ For younger children, let them choose an animal sticker or another symbol that they can easily recognize to place by their name.

▶ Make two sets of name cards. Put one set around the table and have the children match the second one as they find their seat.

▶ Use the name cards for songs or other classroom activities such as working in centers.

 LET'S EAT ▶▶▶▶▶▶▶

Please and Thank You

When?

Help children learn common courtesies they can use at meals and throughout the day.

Why?

Good manners enable children to be accepted in different social situations.

What?

No materials are needed.

How?

➤ Talk about manners and why it is important to be polite.

➤ Help the children understand the connection between their behavior and how others perceive them by role-playing and using puppets to act out classroom situations.

➤ Discuss when to say "please," "thank you" and "excuse me," then sing the following song to the tune of "My Bonnie Lies Over the Ocean."

There are two magic words
That open any door with ease.
One little word is "thanks."
The other word is "please."

Thank you, thank you,
Thank you and please.
Thank you, thank you,
Thank you and please.

Adaptation

➤ Practice answering the telephone, meeting new people and other social situations which call for good manners.

▶▶▶▶▶▶▶   LET'S EAT   ▶▶▶▶▶▶▶

Table Talk

When?

Encourage casual conversations at meal times with these topics.

Why?

Language development, social relationships and personal skills are enhanced by pleasant conversations at lunch and snack.

What?

No materials are needed.

How?

▶ When sharing snack or meals with the children, remember that eating together is a meaningful experience as well as a wonderful learning time.

▶ Be a good listener.

▶ Let the children guide the conversation, or use one of the following suggested topics.

• Tell the children about when you were a little girl or boy. Share stories about your personal life, pets, hobbies and family. (You need to be a real person to them!)

• Ask them about their birthdays or family vacations.

• Talk about how the food tastes. Is it sweet, salty, hard, soft, etc.?

• Discuss upcoming events at school such as a field trip, party, etc.

• Ask them about their families, pets, customs and cultures. Emphasize how we are very much alike, but also different.

• Relate conversations to a theme, a story or other school activity.

• Ask the children about what they like best or least about school.

• Engage children in problem-solving a difficulty in the classroom.

• Talk about wishes, dreams, nightmares and other feelings.

• Listen, listen, listen to what they have to say!

►►►►►►► LET'S EAT ►►►►►►►

Self-Serve Snack

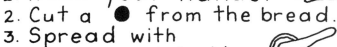

Spider Sandwich

1. Wash your hands.
2. Cut a ● from the bread.
3. Spread with
     peanut butter.
4. Add raisin eyes.
5. Get 8 pretzels. Add for legs.

When?

Let children occasionally serve themselves for morning or afternoon snack.

Why?

Children become independent and responsible by preparing their own snacks. Additionally, they will be using math and reading skills.

What?

trays
utensils
food
picture chart

Preparation

► Place food on trays, along with necessary utensils.

► Make a picture chart illustrating how to prepare the snack.

How?

► At circle time or when children are in a large group, explain what they are having for snack and how to prepare it.

► Allow two to four children at a time to fix their snacks and eat them.

Adaptations

► Draw/write the directions on cards that will stand up.

► Color popsicle sticks with markers. Place the correct number of sticks in a cup next to each food to indicate how many servings each child may take.

► Put a list of children's names by the snack table so they can check themselves off after they've had a turn, or make a bar graph that children can color in when they've eaten.

 NAP TIME

Sandman Dust

When?

Send children to dream land with a little help from the Sandman.

Why?

It is helpful for children to view rest time as a positive experience and to learn how to relax their bodies.

What?

small jewelry box

How?

➤ Tell the children as they lie down on their cots that you'll come sprinkle some of the Sandman's dust on them to help them dream sweet dreams.

➤ Open the box and pretend to dust the children with the contents as you go around the room.

➤ Wait for the children to lie quietly and close their eyes before "sprinkling" them with the dust.

Adaptations

➤ At Christmas time, sprinkle a little green or red glitter on the floor while the children rest, then tell them the elves came in the room and peeked at them while they napped.

➤ Whisper a word of encouragement or a special message in each child's ear at nap time.

Sleepy Time Friends

When?

Sleepy Time Friends come out at nap time to rest with the children.

Why?

These soft toys give children comfort, security and something to hold on to as they relax and rest.

What?

tube socks
polyester filling
rubber bands
markers, felt scraps, pompoms, yarn, wiggly eyes
scissors
glue

Preparation

▶ Take a handful of the filling, wad it up in a ball, then stick it down into the toe of the sock. Twist a rubber band around it.

▶ Make one or two smaller balls in the sock as shown.

▶ Roll down the top of the sock to make a hat.

▶ Decorate it with pompoms, wiggly eyes, felt scraps, etc. to make animals or people.

How?

▶ Let the children keep their little stuffed toys in their cubbies.

▶ When it's time for nap, they can get out their Sleepy Time Friends.

Adaptations

▶ Encourage children to name their toys.

▶ Allow children to bring blankets or other stuffed animals from home for rest time.

Cloud Ride

When?

Take the children for a Cloud Ride when it's time to relax for rest or whenever they seem stressed.

Why?

Visual imagery encourages children to use their imaginations.

What?

tape or record of peaceful music

How?

► Begin playing the music.

► Ask the children to close their eyes.

► Lower your voice and talk slowly as you say the following.

We're going to take a cloud ride.
Hop on a white, fluffy cloud.
Here we go up in the blue sky.
Do you feel the wind in your face?
It's so peaceful up here.
Let your cloud take you to a place where
  you are happy.
Imagine where you are.
Think about who is with you.
You feel so good.
Dream sweet dreams.

Adaptations

► Have the children imagine they are sitting on the beach in the sand listening to the waves break on the shore.

► Let the children ride on a magic carpet, sail on a ship and take other imaginary adventures.

► Play tapes of environmental sounds such as a rain forest, the ocean, the woods, etc. for the children at rest time.

Tighten-Relax

When?

Use this activity to calm children before nap time.

Why?

Tighten-Relax helps children recognize parts of the body as well as release stress.

What?

tape or record of classical music (Baroque works best.)

How?

► Have the children lie on their backs with their eyes closed.

► Turn off the lights and play the classical music.

► With the children, work through the following exercise.

Wiggle your toes. Tighten them up very tight. Tighter. Now let them relax.
Wiggle your feet. Tighten them up very tight. Tighter. Now let them relax.

Wiggle your legs....
Wiggle your hands...
Wiggle your arms...
Wiggle your neck...
Wiggle your head...
Wiggle your whole body...
Your body feels warm and good all over.
It is now ready to rest.

Adaptations

► Have the children squeeze different parts of their bodies like lemons, then relax them.

► Tell the children to stretch various parts of the body.

► Try this breathing exercise with children.

Pretend you are a balloon.
Blow yourself way up.
Bigger, bigger!
Now slowly let out all of the air.
Put your hands on your tummy.
Now blow it up with air.
Do you feel it getting bigger and bigger?
Now slowly let out all of the air.

 NAP TIME

Nocturnal Animals

When?

This activity offers a unique way to help children prepare for nap time.

Why?

Children will develop positive feelings about the dark and rest time.

What?

pictures of nocturnal animals such as bats, mice, owls, wolves, opossums, raccoons, etc. (Look in nature magazines or let the children draw or paint their own animals.)
tape
flashlight

How?

► Talk about what nocturnal animals are and why they only come out at night.

► Show the pictures to the children and encourage them to name the animals and tell about their habits.

► Tape these pictures around the room.

► After turning off the lights for rest, tell the children if they're quiet the nocturnal animals might come out.

► Go around the room and shine the flashlight on the different animals, or let the children quietly take turns finding animals with the flashlight.

Adaptation

► Ask parents to take their child on a nighttime walk. Children can become aware of their senses and talk about how the night feels, what sounds they hear, what they smell, etc.

 NAP TIME ▶▶▶▶▶▶▶

Early Risers

When?

Children who do not sleep or those who wake early will enjoy these activities.

Why?

Children have different sleep needs. Offer those who are awake the choice of an alternative quiet activity.

What?

table toys (puzzles, beads, pegboard, etc.)
listening station (tapes and books)
open art (markers, collage materials, scissors, etc.)
books and magazines

How?

▶ After children have been given ample opportunity to sleep or rest (state licensing standards may specify this), ask them softly if they would like to go to the quiet table to work.

Adaptations

▶ Let one teacher take the children who wake early into another room to play games or do activities.

▶ Set out a self-serve snack for children who wake early.

▶ Prepare a nap time basket with lacing cards, play dough, blank books and markers and other quiet activities children can do on their cots.

Beautiful Bathroom

When?

Children won't need to be reminded to use the bathroom when it is decorated and attractive.

Why?

The bathroom is just an extension of the learning environment and should be pleasant and interesting. In addition, if children have been involved in decorating it, they will be more inclined to keep it clean.

What?

twinkle lights
children's paintings, murals, artwork
rug

Preparation

➤ Decorate the bathroom ceiling with twinkle lights or other seasonal decorations.

➤ Place children's paintings, murals and artwork on the walls at eye level.

➤ Put a rug on the floor to make it more cozy.

How?

➤ Engage the children in decorating the bathroom.

➤ Listen to their input, and let them make the artwork to hang in the bathroom.

➤ Discuss how to care for the bathroom and keep it clean.

Adaptations

➤ Rotate decorations and artwork frequently.

➤ Keep a basket of books or magazines in the bathroom for children to look at.

GAMES

Children love the challenge of games! Games enhance children's language, social skills, motor development and other cognitive abilities while they're playing and having fun. Before lunch, while waiting to change activities or at other in-between times, games can be used to focus children's attention and pull the group together. Indeed, the promise of a game may be just the incentive children need to finish cleaning up and hurry to the rug for circle time. As with all the activities in this book, adapt them to the abilities and interests of the children in your class. Emphasize the joy of playing, rather than winning or losing, and always stop before children become bored or disinterested.

 COLOR GAMES

I Spy

When?

Play this game at circle time, on the bus when going on a field trip, while waiting for lunch or at other times to focus children's attention.

Why?

This game reinforces colors and other concepts.

What?

No materials are needed.

How?

▶ Ask the children to sit on the floor or in chairs.

▶ One child is "it" and says, "I spy something (a color)."

▶ The other children raise their hands and name objects that color.

▶ The first child to correctly identify the object that "it" had in mind becomes the new "it."

Adaptations

▶ Play I Spy with shapes, for example, "I spy something round like a circle."

▶ With older children play I Spy to reinforce letter sounds, for example, "I Spy something that starts with the 'm' sound."

 COLOR GAMES

Categories

When?

Here's a chant to follow circle time or keep children's attention focused.

Why?

This chant provides opportunities for children to develop classification and language skills.

What?

No materials are needed.

How?

► Children sit on the floor or in chairs.

► They slap and snap along to this beat.

Slap, slap (slap thighs)
Snap, snap. (snap left hand, then right)
Slap, slap
Snap, snap.

► When everyone has caught on to the beat, begin the following chant.

Let's play (slap, slap, snap, snap)
Categories. (slap, slap, snap, snap)
Think of (name a category such as colors, animals, fruits, etc.)(continue beat)
Here we go. (child's name)

► Go around the group with everyone adding a word to the category on the "snap, snap."

Adaptation

► Use categories that relate to a theme or concept the children are learning.

Mousie, Mousie

When?

Play this game while lining up or while waiting for the next activity.

Why?

Children enjoy being leaders and choosing friends.

What?

No materials are needed.

How?

► Say the following with the children.

Mousie, mousie,
How quiet can you be?
When I clap my hands,
One-two-three,
We shall see. (clap three times, then call on a quiet child)

► The first time, the teacher selects a child.

► Then that child selects the next child, and so on.

Adaptation

► Play Copy Cat while waiting for a new activity to begin. Say the chant below. Everyone does what the person named does.

Let's play Copy Cat just for fun.
Let's copy (child's name). She's the one.
Whatever she does, we'll do the same.
And that's how you play the Copy Cat game.

 COOPERATION GAMES

Tick-Tack-Toe

When?

Here's a game for a rainy day or with a small group of children.

Why?

Children learn how to cooperate as a team.

What?

masking tape
red and black construction paper
scissors

Preparation

► Make a large tick-tack-toe board on the floor with masking tape.

► Cut out five large black "X's" and five large red "O's" from the construction paper.

How?

► Divide the class into two teams—the "X's" and the "O's."

► Give the first five players on each team an "X" or "O."

► Let the first "X" put her mark on the board.

► Then let the first "O" come and put her mark on the board.

► Continue until each child has had a turn. The object of the game is to get three "X's" or three "O's" in a row diagonally or in a straight line.

Adaptations

► Let children play tick-tack-toe on a chalkboard.

► Ask each child a question which she must answer before placing her "X" or "O" on the board.

 COOPERATION GAMES

Skyscraper

When?

Here's a group game that the whole class will have fun playing.

Why?

Children use small motor skills, as well as thinking skills, when they play this game.

What?

blocks

How?

► Ask the children to sit on the floor in a circle.

► Pass out a block to each child.

► The first child puts his block in the middle of the floor.

► The second child stacks her block on top.

► The game continues with each child carefully placing a block on top as a tall skyscraper is built.

► When the blocks fall down, just begin the game over again.

Adaptations

► Count how many blocks the children can stack before it falls.

► One at a time, let children set the blocks up like dominoes, then knock them over.

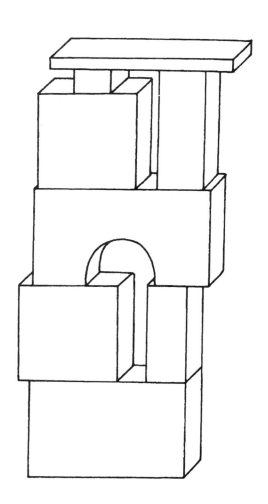

 COOPERATION GAMES

Surprise Pictures

When?

Here's an interesting group project to extend circle time.

Why?

Children cooperate to create surprise pictures.

What?

paper
crayons

How?

➤ Children sit in a circle.

➤ Give each child a piece of paper.

➤ Ask each child to write her name on the back, then begin drawing a picture.

➤ After several minutes, tell the children to stop and pass their papers to the person on their right.

➤ Tell the children to continue drawing on the new picture.

➤ Then tell them to stop again after several minutes and pass the picture on.

➤ Continue drawing and passing until the pictures reach their original owner or time runs out.

➤ The end results are always a big surprise!

Adaptation

➤ Play music, and when the music stops, the children must pass on their pictures.

 LISTENING GAMES

Yes or No

When?

Keep "yes-no" cards handy to focus children's attention for five or ten minutes.

Why?

Children learn to listen and respond to oral questions.

What?

index cards or paper cut in 3" x 5" rectangles
paper clips
markers

Preparation

▶ Write "yes" on one card and "no" on another card. (Each child needs a set.)

▶ Paper-clip the set together.

How?

▶ Pass out a set of cards to each child.

▶ Ask the children various questions to which they must respond by holding up "yes" or "no."

▶ Ask questions about the day, about a story, about their families, about their friends, about numbers, etc.

Adaptation

▶ For little ones, draw a smiling face on one card and a frown on the other card.

LISTENING GAMES

Baby Birds

When?

Lower the noise level in the room or keep children occupied while waiting to begin a new activity.

Why?

Children need to use auditory discrimination skills to find their Baby Birds.

What?

No materials are needed.

How?

▶ Children sit on the floor or in chairs.

▶ One child is selected to be "mama bird" or "papa bird" and leave the room.

▶ While this child is out of the room, five other children are chosen to be baby birds.

▶ All the children put their heads down and the mama or papa bird is called back in the room.

▶ The baby birds then begin "chirping" as mama or papa goes around and tries to identify who they are.

▶ When all the baby birds have been found, begin another round of the game.

Adaptation

▶ Use different animals to play this game. Pretend to be puppies, kittens, cubs, etc.

 LISTENING GAMES

Hot Potato

When?

Play this "hot" game just for fun or to dismiss children from a group activity.

Why?

Children learn to listen and develop motor skills as they play Hot Potato.

What?

beanbag
music (tape or record)

How?

➤ Have the children sit in a circle and begin passing the beanbag around as the music is played.

➤ Stop the music.

➤ Whoever is holding the beanbag is out of the game. (That child can just scoot back from the circle or can be dismissed to another activity.)

➤ The game continues until there is one child left.

Adaptations

➤ Pass a real potato, stuffed animal, small ball or other object.

➤ Let children name rhyming words, favorite foods, pets or other categories if they are caught holding the beanbag when the music stops.

➤ Play this game out on the playground, but instead of having the children sit, let them stand in a circle. Blow a whistle instead of stopping music.

 LISTENING GAMES

Missing Child

When?

Looking for the missing child will quietly keep children's attention.

Why?

This game contributes to children's self-esteem and helps them develop descriptive skills.

What?

No materials are needed.

How?

➤ Children sit on the floor or in chairs.

➤ Tell them they are looking for a lost child.

➤ Begin describing a child in the room by hair color, clothing and other individual characteristics.

➤ When a child thinks he knows who the missing child is, he raises his hand or puts his finger on his nose.

➤ When each child has his or her hand up or finger on his or her nose, the missing child stands up and says, "Here I am!"

➤ This "missing child" then becomes the detective, describing another friend.

➤ The game continues until everyone has had a turn or time runs out.

Adaptation

➤ Let one child be detective and leave the room. Select another child to hide in a corner of the room. When the detective returns, he tries to identify the missing child.

 LISTENING GAMES

Simon Says

When?

Simon Says is more than a game—it's a wonderful way to get children's attention.

Why?

Children develop auditory skills as they listen and follow directions.

What?

No materials are needed.

How?

▶ Teach children how to play Simon Says by telling them they should only follow a command if it is proceeded by the words "Simon Says."

▶ They will need to listen carefully.

▶ They should not do anything if Simon doesn't tell them to do it.

▶ As the game is played, children who do something that Simon doesn't tell them to do are out of the game and must sit down.

Adaptation

▶ Play Simon Says at various times in the day to prepare children for new activities or to move them through the day. For example, while lining the children up on the playground, say, "Simon says put your hands on your head. Simon says touch your toes. Simon says face forward and walk in a quiet line to get a drink of water."

 LISTENING GAMES

Diddle, Diddle Dumpling

When?

This game entertains a group on a rainy day or when there are a few minutes to spare.

Why?

Children have fun guessing who took their shoe.

What?

No materials are needed.

How?

➤ Have the children sit in a circle.

➤ Choose one child to be "John."

➤ John takes off one shoe and puts it in the middle of the circle.

➤ "John" then hides in a corner and closes his eyes.

➤ Point to a child who takes "John's" shoe and hides it in his lap.

➤ Say the verse below.

Diddle, diddle, dumpling,
My son, John,
Went to bed
With his trousers on.
One shoe off
And the other shoe on.
Diddle, diddle, dumpling,
My son, John.

Hey, John,
Your shoe is gone.
When you find it
You put it on.
Hey, John,
Your shoe is gone.
Find it now,
And put it on.

➤ The children yell, "Wake up, John."

➤ "John" returns to the circle and tries to guess who has his shoe.

➤ He gets three guesses.

➤ The person who took the shoe becomes the new "John."

 MATH GAMES

Hands Up

When?

Use this game while waiting to change activities or with a small group.

Why?

The children learn mathematical skills.

What?

construction paper
markers
scissors
envelopes

Preparation

- ▶ Cut the construction paper into 3" squares. Each child needs five squares.

- ▶ Print the numbers 1-5 on the squares. Print an equal number of dots on each card. For example, the number 1 card has one dot on it, the number 2 card has two dots on it, etc.

- ▶ Put a set of numeral cards in each envelope.

How?

- ▶ The children sit on the floor or at tables.

- ▶ Give each child an envelope.

- ▶ Tell the children to spread the cards out in front of them.

- ▶ Call out different numerals.

- ▶ The children find them and hold them up. (With a sweep of your eyes, you can tell who has grasped each concept.)

- ▶ With older children, clap your hands, and ask the children to hold up a card to represent the number of claps.

Adaptations

- ▶ With younger children, use three numbers.

- ▶ Give older children the numerals 0-10 or higher.

- ▶ Make Hands Up cards using shapes, colors or letters.

 MATH GAMES

Four Corners

When?

Give children the opportunity to get up and move around between activities with Four Corners.

Why?

This is a game of luck that everyone will want to participate in.

What?

No materials are needed.

How?

▶ Number each of the corners in the room—1, 2, 3 and 4.

▶ Choose one person to be "it."

▶ He hides his eyes.

▶ As "it" counts slowly from one to ten, everyone else tiptoes to a corner in the room.

▶ When "it" says "freeze," everyone must be in a corner.

▶ "It" then calls out the number of a corner (1, 2, 3 or 4) and the children in that corner are out of the game and must sit down in the "stew pot" in the middle of the room.

▶ "It" begins counting to ten again as everyone moves to a new corner.

▶ The game continues until there is one person left, and that person then becomes the new "it."

Adaptation

▶ Shorten the game by having "it" call out two corners at a time.

Round-Up

When?

Rather than having children wait and become bored, involve them in this matching game.

Why?

Children get up and move around while practicing visual discrimination skills.

What?

construction paper (different colors)
scissors
markers
ziplock bag

Preparation

▶ Use the pattern to cut out 10-25 pairs of boots from construction paper. Each child will need one pair of boots, so cut out as many pairs as there are children in the class.

▶ Using markers, decorate each pair of boots with designs and colors so they are different from the others.

▶ Store the boots in a ziplock bag.

How?

▶ Separate the pairs of boots.

▶ Have the children sit in a circle.

▶ Give each child a boot.

▶ Tell the children to close their eyes.

▶ Hide the other boots around the room in plain sight.

▶ Say, "Round-Up."

▶ The children go around the room, trying to find their matching boot.

▶ After finding their boot, they sit back down.

Adaptation

▶ Let the children take turns hiding the boots.

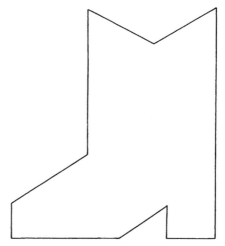

 MEMORY GAMES

The Quiet Touch

When?

Children will enjoy this game whenever there are a few extra minutes.

Why?

Visual memory and sequence skills are developed.

What?

No materials are needed.

How?

▶ The first child gets up, touches an object in the room, then sits down.

▶ The second child gets up, touches what the first child touched, touches a second object, then sits down.

▶ The game continues with each child touching the objects the previous children touched in sequential order, plus a new object at the end.

▶ When a child misses, just begin a new game.

Adaptations

▶ Children enjoy the challenge of counting and seeing how many objects they can remember.

▶ A similar game can be played with children making various noises. When playing Noisy Touch, children might turn on the sink, shut the door, write on the board, move a chair, etc. Each child adds a new sound until the sequence is missed, then begin again.

 MEMORY GAMES

Concentration

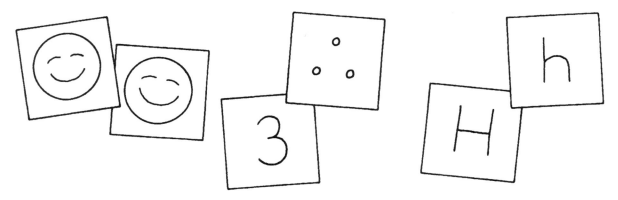

When?

This game focuses children's attention in a quiet way.

Why?

Concentration gives children an excellent opportunity to develop visual memory skills.

What?

poster board
markers

Preparation

▶ Cut twelve squares that measure 6" from the poster board.

▶ Draw similar pictures or shapes on pairs of cards. Use stickers, coupons, road signs or seasonal symbols.

How?

▶ Have children sit in a circle on the floor.

▶ Spread the cards out in the middle of the circle face down.

▶ One at a time, children come up and turn over two cards.

▶ If the cards match, the child keeps them and has another turn.

▶ If the cards don't match, the cards are turned back over and the next child gets a turn.

▶ Continue playing the game until all the pairs are matched.

Adaptations

▶ Vary the number of cards used according to the ability of the children.

▶ Write upper and lowercase letters, sight words and more difficult information on the cards for older children.

▶ Let two children or small groups play this game independently.

 MEMORY GAMES

Mystery Blanket

When?

This is a quick game that entertains children while waiting to change activities.

Why?

Mystery Blanket encourages visual memory skills and can be adapted for all ages.

What?

baby blanket, scarf or towel
4 objects (toys, crayons, eating utensils or other classroom items)

How?

▶ Lay the objects on the floor.

▶ Ask the children to name them.

▶ Tell the children to take a picture of the things in their minds and then close their eyes.

▶ Lay the blanket over the items, and carefully slide one of the objects behind your back.

▶ Have the children open their eyes, then lift the blanket and see who can tell which object is missing.

▶ Select one child to identify the missing object, or let all the children whisper the answer at the same time.

Adaptations

▶ Increase the number of objects according to the ability of the group.

▶ Play a similar memory game using felt pieces on the flannel board.

 MEMORY GAMES

Going on a Picnic

When?

Play this game whenever there are a few extra minutes.

Why?

Auditory memory and sequence skills are developed as children play.

What?

No materials are needed.

How?

► Have the children sit in a circle.

► The first child says "I'm going on a picnic and I'm taking a (name of a food)."

► The second child says, "I'm going on a picnic and I'm taking (names first object)" and adds another item.

► The third child repeats what the first two children said, plus another item.

► The game proceeds with each child adding another object she would take on the picnic.

► When a child can't remember, simply begin the game all over again.

Adaptation

► Change the game to going on a trip to the moon, packing Santa's sleigh and other imaginary visits.

In the Bag

When?

In the Bag extends group time and involves children of different ages.

Why?

This game reinforces letter recognition and sounds.

What?

small grocery sack
poster board
scissors
markers

Preparation

► Cut the poster boards into 26 3" squares.

► On each square print a letter of the alphabet.

► Put the squares in the grocery sack.

How?

► Have the children sit in a circle.

► One at a time let the children take the bag, draw a card, identify the letter and tell something they would buy that begins with that sound.

► Continue the game until all the children have had a turn or you run out of time.

Adaptations

► For younger children, cut pictures of food and other grocery store items and glue them to the cards. They will be delighted to choose a card and identify the food on it.

► Challenge older children by asking them to think of a word in a specific category such as clothing, fruits, pets, etc.

Go Fishing

When?

Play this game with a small group any time during the day.

Why?

Many learning skills are reinforced with this simple game format.

What?

construction paper
yarn or string
stick (A stick from a tree works well.)
paper clips
horseshoe magnet

Preparation

▶ Using the pattern, cut out 10-25 fish from the construction paper.

▶ Attach a paper clip to each fish and print numerals, letters or words on the fish.

▶ Tie a piece of string or yarn 2-3 feet long to the end of the stick. Then tie the magnet to the other end of the string.

How?

▶ Spread the fish out on the floor.

▶ One at a time, let the children take the fishing pole and try to catch a fish by hooking the magnet to the paper clip on the fish.

▶ Let each child identify the information on her fish, then pass the fishing pole to a friend.

Jumping Beans

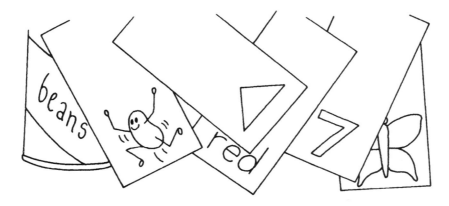

When?

Use this game to reinforce skills at circle time or when there are a few extra minutes.

Why?

Children get to "jump and jiggle" as they learn.

What?

large, empty bean can with label still on. (Be sure the top edge is smooth. Cover with cloth tape if necessary.)
poster board or heavy paper
markers
scissors

Preparation

▶ Cut the poster board into 25 strips that measure 6" x 2-1/2".

▶ On the bottom of five strips draw a little bean.

▶ On the bottom of the other strips draw letters, numerals, shapes, etc.

▶ Put all the strips in the bean can with the information at the bottom.

How?

▶ Ask the children to sit in a circle.

▶ One at a time, the children take the can, pull out a strip and identify the information on the bottom.

▶ If a child draws a bean, she calls out "jumping beans!"

▶ Everyone must stand up and jump up and down.

▶ Continue passing the can around the circle until each child has had a turn.

Adaptation

▶ Vary the information on the strips to reinforce a concept or theme the children are learning.

Dogs and Bones

When?

This game is good for large and small groups to keep children occupied.

Why?

Colors, letters, sets, numerals and other information are reinforced.

What?

construction paper
scissors
markers
ziplock bag

Preparation

➤ Using the pattern, cut out a dog and bone for each child.

➤ Choose one of the following ideas for the cutouts:

Dogs and bones of the same color.
Dogs and bones with matching shapes.
Dogs and bones with upper and lowercase letters.
Numerals on the dogs and matching sets on the bones.

➤ Store the pieces in the ziplock bag.

How?

➤ Have the children sit on the floor.

➤ Give each child a dog.

➤ Tell the children to close their eyes.

➤ Hide the bones around the room in plain sight.

➤ Explain that the dogs have hidden their bones, but they can't remember where they are.

➤ Ask the children to help the dogs hunt for their bones.

Adaptations

➤ Choose other ideas or concepts to reinforce what the children are learning.

➤ Use bunnies and carrots, kittens and mittens, baseballs and bats and other matching objects to make similar games.

Elfie

When?

Here's a quick game to use any time during the day.

Why?

Attention span, as well as other skills, are strengthened with the help of Elfie.

What?

poster board
markers
scissors
construction paper
ziplock bag

Preparation

▶ Cut the poster board into twelve rectangles, 6" x 8".

▶ Choose a concept to reinforce such as shapes, colors or numerals and print them on the cards.

▶ Draw an elf, similar to the one shown, on the construction paper and cut it out.

▶ Store all the pieces in the ziplock bag.

How?

▶ Let the children sit on the floor in a circle.

▶ Place the cards on the floor.

▶ Ask the children to name the information on the cards.

▶ Introduce Elfie as a little elf who likes to hide and trick people.

▶ Next, have the children turn their backs and close their eyes.

▶ Hide Elfie under one of the cards.

▶ When they turn around, choose one child to guess where she thinks Elfie is hiding, and then look under that card.

▶ When Elfie is found, that child may hide him as the others turn their backs and close their eyes.

Adaptations

▶ Use fewer cards for younger children.

▶ Vary the character who hides under the cards to relate to a theme or holiday. Hide a bunny, bear, valentine, etc.

Flash

When?

Play Flash when there are a few extra minutes until it's time to dismiss children to another activity.

Why?

Skills and concepts are fun to learn if they are practiced by using games.

What?

flash cards of colors, animals, shapes, etc. (Purchase these or make your own by writing the information on index cards with markers.)

How?

► Flash the cards in front of the children and let them all whisper the answer.

► To dismiss children one at a time, go around the circle and have children individually identify the information on the cards.

► Always allow children to succeed, prompting them with the correct answer if they need help.

Adaptation

► Let children play with the flash cards in pairs. Have them place the cards face down on the floor in front of them. They turn over one card at a time and identify the information on it. If they answer correctly, they may keep the card.

A B C Stretch

When?

If children are full of wiggles or they need a break, then do the alphabet stretch.

Why?

Fill their lungs with air while building reading readiness skills.

What?

No materials are needed.

How?

► Have the children stand, stretch their hands in the air and say "A."

► Touch shoulders and say "B."

► Touch toes and say "C."

► Continue with the letters of the alphabet, stretching a different way for each letter.

Adaptations

► With younger children, use just a few letters.

► With older children, ask them to whisper a word that begins with each letter.

▶▶▶▶▶▶   THINKING GAMES   ▶▶▶▶▶▶

Who's the Leader?

When?

Here's a good game to keep children busy while waiting to begin a new activity.

Why?

Children sharpen their visual discrimination skills as they try to discover the mysterious leader.

What?

No materials are needed.

How?

▶ Begin the game by having the children sit in a circle.

▶ One child is chosen to leave the room.

▶ While he is out in the hall, another child is chosen to be the mystery leader.

▶ The mystery leader will make different hand and facial motions as the rest of the group carefully watches and follows along. The mystery leader might clap, slap thighs, touch shoulders, blink eyes, etc.

▶ The child in the hall is called back in the room.

▶ He stands in the middle of the circle and tries to figure out who the mystery leader is.

▶ The game proceeds with other children taking turns going out in the hall and being mystery leader.

▶▶▶▶▶▶ 9 ▶▶▶▶▶▶

POCKETFUL OF SONGS

People sing because they're happy, and they're happy because they sing. So keep a song in your pocket to pull the class together, release stress and brighten spirits. Music offers a positive way to teach letters, numbers and other concepts, but more importantly, it's an activity that allows every child to experience success.

If your mind goes "blank" when you need a song to sing, keep a little list in your pocket, or ask the children if they have a favorite song to sing. Post a language experience chart of the class's favorite songs to prompt you.

Connect with the joy of childhood and enhance it with the songs and props in this chapter. And don't worry if you can't carry a tune—your enthusiasm will more than make up for any missed notes!

Fishing Song

When?

Stand up and shake the wiggles out with this song.

Why?

Concepts of loud, soft, fast and slow are introduced with the Fishing Song.

What?

No materials are needed.

How?

▶ Put hands over heads and get ready to fish.

▶ Sing the following to the tune of "Turkey in the Straw."

Have you ever (hands over head)
Been a fishing (pretend to throw out line)
On a bright (make a circle with arms around your head like a sun)
And sunny day?
When you see (put hands together and wiggle like a fish)
Those little fishes
Swimming up (wiggle hands from side to side)
And down the bay?

With their hands (put hands on hips in front)
In their pockets,
And their pockets (put hands on hips in back)
In their pants,
All the little fishes (put hands on waist and wiggle hips as if dancing)
Do the Wiggle Wiggle dance.

Adaptations

▶ Sing the song slowly with slow motions, then sing it fast with quick motions.

▶ Use a loud voice, then a soft voice to sing the song.

▶ Leave out two lines at a time, just humming the words and doing the motions, until everyone is humming the whole song.

The Bear Went Over the Mountain

When?

Sing this song while waiting for an activity to begin.

Why?

Children practice sequencing and language skills as they sing along.

What?

No materials are needed.

How?

▶ This song is a fun twist to an old favorite.

The bear went over the mountain.
The bear went over the mountain.
The bear went over the mountain.
And what do you think he saw?

He saw a plate of brownies.
He saw a plate of brownies.
He saw a plate of brownies.
And what do you think he did?

He ate up all the brownies, etc. ...
He got a tummy ache, etc. ...
He took some Alka Seltzer, etc. ...
He went and told his mommy, etc. ...
She sent him to his room, etc. ...

He never went over the mountain.
He never went over the mountain.
He never went over the mountain.
To see what he could see.

Adaptations

▶ Make a big book for this song, letting two or three children illustrate each verse. Use poster board or large grocery sacks for the pages.

▶ Do a language experience chart based on this song. Let each child dictate a sentence about what she thinks the bear saw on the other side of the mountain.

I Wish I Were

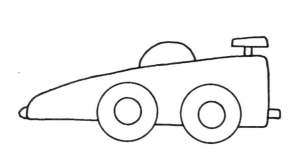  

When?

Use this entertaining song to fill a few extra minutes.

Why?

This song encourages children's imagination.

What?

No materials are needed.

How?

➤ Sing the following verses to the tune of "If You're Happy and You Know It."

Oh, I wish I were a little race car.
I wish I were a little race car.
I'd go zoom, zoom, zoom, zoom, zoom,
Oh, I wish I were a little race car.

Oh, I wish I were a little piece of orange.
I wish I were a little piece of orange.
I'd go squirty, squirty, squirty over every-
body's shirty,
Oh, I wish I were a little piece of orange.

I wish I were a little bit of mud...
I'd go oozie, oozie, oozie in everybody's
tootsies...

I wish I were a little cupcake...
I'd go yummy, yummy, yummy in every-
body's tummy...

I wish I were a little baby fish...
I'd be such a cutey in my little bathing
suity...

I wish I were a little radio...
I'd go click. (Stop singing and "turn off" the
chant.)

Adaptations

➤ Color and cut out a picture to go with each verse of the song.

➤ Glue one picture to a piece of poster board. Hold up the picture for each verse of the song.

➤ Use the pictures to make a book or a flannel board activity.

➤ Let the children make up their own silly verses about what they wish they were and why.

➤ Print the words to each verse on the song cards.

Katalina Matalina

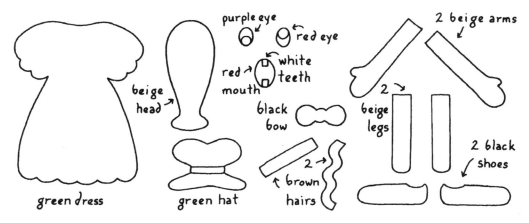

When?

Here's a funny song to lighten spirits and pull the group together.

Why?

Singing builds positive group feelings while enhancing language skills.

What?

felt scraps
scissors
glue
flannel board

Preparation

▶ Draw or trace the patterns (shown in illustration) on felt and cut them out. Enlarge as needed.

▶ Glue the arms and legs to the back of the dress.

How?

▶ Place the dress on the flannel board, then add the other parts of the body while singing the following to the tune of "Shortnin' Bread."

Chorus:
Katalina Matalina Upsadina Walkadina
Hoca Poca Loca was her name.

Her head was shaped like a baseball bat,
And right on top was a funny old hat.
(Chorus)
She had two hairs on her head.
One was alive and the other was dead.
(Chorus)
She had two eyes in her head.
One was purple and the other was red.
(Chorus)
She had two teeth in her mouth.
One pointed north and the other pointed
*   south.*
(Chorus)
Her neck was as long as a ten foot pole.
And right in the middle was a big black bow.
(Chorus)
Her feet were as flat as a bathroom mat.
How did they ever get like that?
(Chorus)

▶▶▶▶▶▶ FUNNY SONGS ▶▶▶▶▶▶

A Sailor Went to Sea

When?

Use this song to let children stretch and wiggle and help them quiet down.

Why?

Children have fun doing the motions as they sing the nonsense words.

What?

No materials are needed.

How?

▶ Stand up straight like sailors, then begin singing.

> A sailor went to sea, sea, sea. (put hand over eye as if saluting)
> To see what he could see, see, see.
> And all that he could see, see, see,
> Was the bottom of the deep blue sea, sea, sea.

> A sailor went to chop, chop, chop. (make chopping motion with arm)
> To see what he could chop, chop, chop.
> And all that he could chop, chop, chop,
> Was the bottom of the deep blue chop, chop, chop.
> A sailor went to knee, knee, knee... (touch knee)
> A sailor went to tap, tap, tap... (tap toe)
> A sailor went to washy-wash... (put hands on hips and wiggle)

▶ For the last verse, put all the motions together.

> A sailor went to sea, chop, knee, tap, washy-wash.
> To see what he could see, chop, knee, tap, washy-wash.
> And all that he could see, chop, knee, tap, washy-wash,
> Was the bottom of the deep blue sea, chop, knee, tap, washy-wash.

▶▶▶▶▶▶   FUNNY SONGS   ▶▶▶▶▶▶

Five Little Ducks

When?

Sing or act out Five Little Ducks in just a few minutes.

Why?

Children enjoy performing, and they will learn number concepts as they sing.

What?

No materials are needed.

How?

▶ Practice singing this song, then select five children to be the baby ducks, one to be momma duck and one to be daddy duck.

Five little ducks (hold up five fingers)
Went out to play (flap arms like wings)
Over the hills (move arm up and down)
And far away. (hand over eyes)
When the momma duck (make beak with hands)
Called, "Quack, quack, quack."
And four little ducks (hold up four fingers)
Came waddling back. (flap arms like wings)

Four little ducks...

▶ Continue singing until there are no little ducks left.

No little ducks
Went out to play
Over the hills
And far away.
When the daddy duck (use both arms to make a big beak)
Called, "QUACK-QUACK-QUACK-QUACK." (say with a loud voice)
Five little ducks
Came waddling back.

Adaptation

▶ Make duck headbands or paper wings for the children to wear as they dramatize the song.

 FUNNY SONGS

Alice the Camel

When?

Sing about Alice while waiting or to release energy.

Why?

This song reinforces number concepts as children exercise.

What?

No materials are needed.

How?

➤ Stand up, put hands on hips and begin to chant the following to the tune of "Dry Bones."

Alice the camel (hands on hips)
Has five humps. (hold up five fingers)
Alice the camel
Has five humps.
Alice the camel
Has five humps.
So go, Alice, go. (cheer with hand)
Boom, boom, boom! (wiggle hips from side
    to side)
Alice the camel
Has four humps...

➤ Count down until the last verse.

Alice the camel (hands on hips)
Has no humps. (hold up 0 fingers)
Alice the camel
Has no humps.
Alice the camel
Has no humps.
Because Alice is a horse! (shout this last line)

Adaptation

➤ Have children stand in a circle with their arms around each other and bump hips on the boom, boom, boom.

Tiny Tim

When?

Tiny Tim, the turtle, keeps little hands busy and captures children's interest.

Why?

Children develop sequencing skills and auditory memory as they sing and imitate the motions.

What?

No materials are needed.

How?

▶ Hold hands cupped together to make a turtle.

▶ Say or chant the following song.

I had a little turtle. (pretend to hold a turtle)
His name was Tiny Tim.
I put him in the bathtub (put in tub)
To see if he could swim. (make swimming motions)
He drank up all the water. (slurp)
He ate up all the soap. (smack lips)
And now he's sick in bed
With bubbles in his throat. (blow bubbles with lips)
B-b-b-b-b!

Mother called the doctor. (hold hand like a phone)
Mother called the nurse.
Mother called the lady
With the alligator purse.

"Measles," said the doctor. (point finger)
"Mumps," said the nurse.
"Nothing," said the lady
With the alligator purse.

"Aspirin," said the doctor. (hold open hand)
"Gargle," said the nurse.
"Nothing," said the lady
With the alligator purse.

Out went the doctor. (wave hand good-bye)
Out went the nurse.
Out went the lady
With the alligator purse.

▶▶▶▶▶▶ FUNNY SONGS ▶▶▶▶▶▶

Over in the Meadow

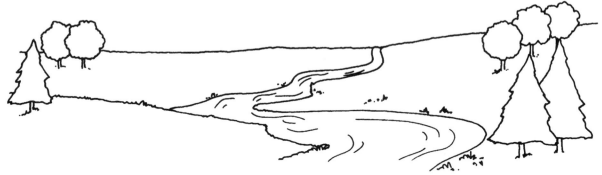

When?

As children are slowly joining the group, begin singing this song to entertain the ones who are there and encourage others to join the group.

Why?

Children learn sets and numbers as they sing along.

What?

poster board
scissors
markers
2 book rings
hole punch

Preparation

▶ To make a step book, cut the poster board into five pieces, each one two inches shorter than the previous one. (For example, 10" x 14", 10" x 12", 10" x 10", 10" x 8" and 10" x 6".)

▶ Number the pages 1-5 and illustrate the verses with markers as shown.

▶ Punch holes in the top of each page and put together with book rings.

How?

▶ Show each page while singing the verses of the song.

Over in the meadow
In the sand and the sun
Lived an old mother frog
And her little froggie one.
"Hop," said the mother.
"I hop," said the one.
So they hopped and were glad
In the sand and the sun.

Over in the meadow
Where the stream runs blue
Lived an old mother fishy
And her little fishies two.
"Swim," said the mother.
"We swim," said the two.
So they swam and were glad
Where the stream runs blue.

Over in the meadow
In a nest in a tree
Lived an old mother red bird
And her little birdies three.
"Fly," said the mother.
"We fly," said the three.
So they flew and were glad
In the nest in the tree.

Over in the meadow
By an old apple core
Lived an old mother wormie
And her little wormies four.
"Squirm," said the mother.
"We squirm," said the four.
So they squirmed and were glad
By the old apple core.

Over in the meadow
By the big beehive
Lived an old mother bee
And her little bees five.
"Buzz," said the mother.
"We buzz," said the five.
So they buzzed and were glad
By the big beehive

Adaptation

➤ Choose children to be the different animals and to act out the song.

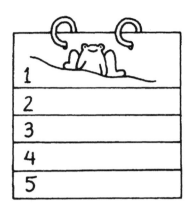

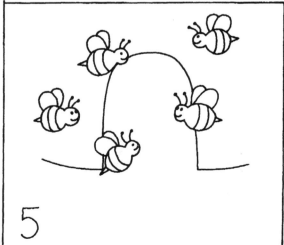

 **FUNNY SONGS** ▶▶▶▶▶▶

My Mother Is a Baker

When?

This is a long chant that keeps children focused between activities or while waiting.

Why?

Sequencing, auditory memory, motor and language skills are practiced in a fun way.

What?

No materials are needed.

How?

▶ Demonstrate the motions and encourage the children to follow along.

My mother is a baker, a baker, a baker.
My mother is a baker.
She always goes like this, "Yum, yum!" (pat tummy)

My father is a trash man, a trash man, a trash man.
My father is a trash man.
He always goes like this, "Yum, yum, Pee yew!" (pat tummy, hold nose)

▶ Continue with the following verses, adding the new motion at the end.

My sister is a singer...
She always goes like this, "La ta de da and a toodle ee doo." (put out hands like an opera singer)

My brother is a cowboy...
He always goes like this, "Giddap!" (pretend to ride horse)

My doggie is a licker...
He always goes like this, "Slurp, slurp." (slurp with tongue)

My kitty is a scratcher...
She always goes like this, "scratch, scratch." (scratch with hands)

My baby is a whiner...
He always goes like this, "Waa, waa." (pretend to cry)

My Grandpa is an engineer...
He always goes like this, "Toot, toot." (pull whistle)

My Grandma is a tickler...
She always goes like this. (end song by tickling each other)

My Aunt Came Back

When?

Wiggle and lighten the mood in the room with this movement song.

Why?

More important than the coordination it takes to sing this song, is the good laugh everyone will have from looking so silly.

What?

No materials are needed.

How?

▶ This is an echo song to the tune of "How Dry I Am." Ask the children to repeat each line as they do the motions.

My aunt came back
From Birmingham
And brought me back
A paper fan. (wave hand like a fan)
My aunt came back from New York, too,
And brought me back
A dancing shoe. (continue waving fan and
*   tap your foot)*

▶ Keep on singing the verses below, adding new motions to the ones you are already doing.

...County fair...rocking chair. (rock back and
*   forth)*
...Miami...itchy flea. (wiggle all over)
...Washington...bubble gum. (pretend to
*   chew gum)*
...City zoo...nuts like you! (point finger at
*   everyone)*

 FUNNY SONGS ▶▶▶▶▶▶

Arm Dance

When?

If children are restless, take a break and release energy with this activity.

Why?

Sequencing and motor skills are developed as children move to the music.

What?

record or tape with a steady rhythm

How?

▶ The children sit in chairs or on the floor.

▶ Ask, "Did you know your arms could dance? What are some different motions your arms could do?"

▶ As the children suggest motions, number them.

▶ Record an illustration of the motion and its number on an experience chart. Motions might include clapping, snapping, slapping, rolling, waving, shaking, touching shoulders, etc.

▶ Play the music and do the motions, keeping to the rhythm. Do each motion for a count of ten.

▶ Start off with two motions, then add others as the children are successful.

Adaptations

▶ Think of other exercises such as sitting, rocking from side to side, touching the floor, leg kicks, etc.

▶ Play music on a fast speed or slow speed, and let the children move accordingly.

▶ Play freeze, by stopping and starting the music. The children dance freely when the music is playing, but must stop and freeze when it stops.

Jack and Jill

When?

Here come Jack and Jill to direct children's attention.

Why?

Nursery rhymes foster children's oral language and their ability to rhyme.

What?

No materials are needed.

How?

▶ Say the rhyme and do the actions.

Jack and Jill (hold up thumbs and pretend to climb)
Went up a hill
To fetch a pail of water.
Jack fell down (drop one thumb down)
And broke his crown,
And Jill came tumbling after.
    (drop other thumb down)
Then up got Jack (hold up one thumb)
And said to Jill (hold other thumb up)
As in his arms he took her, (clasp thumbs)
"You're not hurt, (brush thumbs together)

Brush off that dirt,
And let's go fetch that water."
So Jack and Jill (hold up thumbs and pretend
    to climb up)
Went up a hill
To fetch a pail of water.
They brought it back (climb down)
To mother dear,
Who thanked her son and daughter.
    (fold hands and put in lap)

Adaptations

▶ Trace and cut out the body pattern from heavy paper. You will need two. Draw Jack on one pattern, and Jill on the other pattern. Glue Jack and Jill to the stick, back to back. Say the rhyme with the puppet, turning it back and forth.

▶ Let the children make their own puppets of Jack and Jill.

▶ Give the children the opportunity to act out "Jack and Jill" and other nursery rhymes.

 NURSERY RHYME SONGS

Eensy Weensy Spider

When?

This song keeps little hands busy as children wait for a new activity to begin.

Why?

Loud and soft verses add a new dimension to this old song.

What?

No materials are needed.

How?

▶ Show children how to make a spider by touching thumbs to opposite forefingers and alternating them as they move them up in the air.

The eensy weensy spider (move fingers up—thumbs to opposite forefingers)
Went up the water spout.
Down came the rain (wiggle fingers down like rain)
And washed the spider out.
Out came the sun (make circle over head with arms)
And dried up all the rain.
And the eensy weensy spider (move fingers up)
Went up the spout again.

▶ Say, "Did you know that next door to the eensy weensy spider lived the big, fat spider?"

The big, fat spider (sing with a loud, deep voice)
Went up the water spout.
Down came the rain (make big motions)
And washed the spider out.
Out came the sun (make big circle over head with arms)
And dried up all the rain.
And the big, fat spider (clap hands to make the big spider)
Went up the spout again.

▶ Say, "And did you know that on the other side of the eensy weensy spider lived the teensy, weensy spider?"

The teensy weensy spider (sing with a high, soft voice; make a tiny spider with fingers)
Went up the water spout.
Down came the rain (make small motions)
And washed the spider out.
Out came the sun (make tiny circle)
And dried up all the rain.
And the teensy weensy spider (make tiny spider climb up again)
Went up the spout again.

 NURSERY RHYME SONGS

Hickory Dickory Dock

When?

This rhyme will catch children's attention with its rhythm and help focus their attention for a group activity.

Why?

Children's counting and motor skills are reinforced as they sing along.

What?

No materials are needed.

How?

➤ Put hands together in front.

➤ Move them slowly back and forth when saying, "Tick-tock, tick-tock."

Hickory, dickory, dock (move hands back and forth)
The mouse ran up the clock. (run fingers above head)
The clock struck one, (clap once above head)
The mouse ran down. (run fingers down)
Hickory, dickory, dock.
Tick-tock, tick-tock.

➤ Continue with these other verses.

...The clock struck two, (clap hands twice)
The mouse said, "Boo!"
...The clock struck three, (clap hands three times)
The mouse said, "Whee!"
...The clock struck four, (clap hands four times)
The mouse said, "No more."

Adaptation

➤ Make up verses for other numbers such as "The clock struck five, the mouse said, 'Let's jive!'"

PUPPET SONGS

Ten in the Bed

When?

Grab children's attention with the prop for this song. Start the song and challenge children to finish cleaning up and join circle time (or anytime) before the last bear falls off the bed!

Why?

While children are singing along they learn numerals and about subtraction.

What?

file folder
construction paper
markers
scissors
brad fastener
tape
piece of fabric 14" x 10"

Preparation

➤ Color the bears and cut out the pillow.

➤ Draw the head post of a bed on the top half of the file folder. Tape the piece of fabric to the bottom half to resemble a quilt on the bed.

➤ Attach the bears and pillow with a brad to the center bottom of the top half.

How?

➤ Ask the children to hold up ten fingers.

➤ Open the file folder and count the ten bears in the bed.

➤ Begin the song, turning the wheel to make a bear disappear after each verse.

There were ten in the bed (hold up ten fingers)
And the little one said,
"Roll over, roll over." (roll hands)
So they all rolled over
And one fell out. (hold up nine fingers)
There were nine in the bed (hold up nine fingers)
And the little one said... (continue until there is one bear left)
There was one in the bed
And the little one said,
"I've got the whole bed to myself."

(Clap hands and sing the following to the tune of "He's Got the Whole World in His Hands.")

"I've got the whole bed to myself.
I've got the whole bed to myself.
I've got the whole bed to myself."

Adaptations

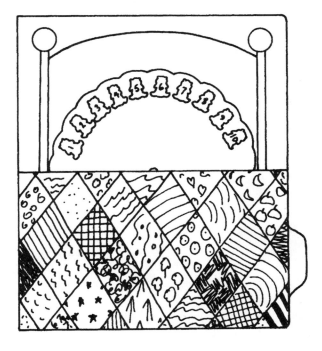

▶ Let children act out this song by pretending that they are the little bears, rolling away and sitting down as the song is sung.

▶ Sing the reverse of this song. "There was one in the bed and the little one said, 'I'm lonely. I'm lonely.' So he rolled over and one came back. There were two in the bed," etc.

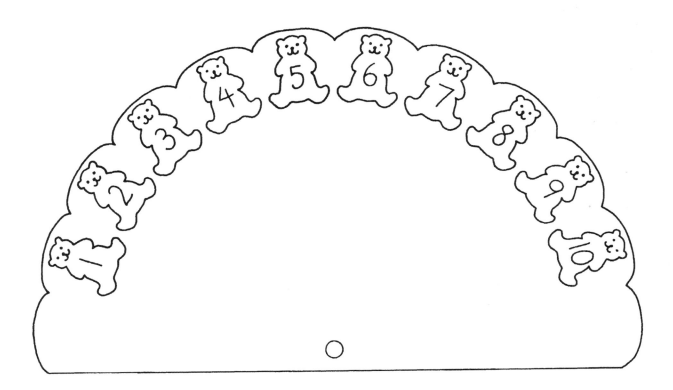

Michael Finnegan

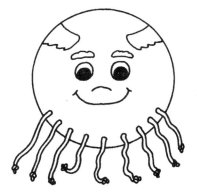 

When?

The prop for this song is sure to get children's attention. Sing the song over and over until all the children join in.

Why?

Visuals help focus children's attention.

What?

paper plate
crayons, markers, scissors
8 pieces of yarn—each 10" long

Preparation

► Decorate the paper plate to resemble the face of Michael Finnegan.

► Make eight small holes with a pencil point on the bottom of the plate and thread one yarn piece through each hole.

► Tie all the ends of yarn together in the back of the paper plate to keep them from sliding back through the holes. Then tie a knot at the other end of each piece of yarn on the front side.

How?

► Start with all the yarn pulled to the back of the plate.

► As you sing the song, pull the yarn whiskers through to the front of the face one by one.

I knew a man named Michael Finnegan.
He had whiskers on his chinegan.
The wind blew them off, (pull the knot of yarn in the back to make the whiskers disappear, then pull them out again in front)
But they grew in again.
Poor old Michael Finnegan.
Begin again.

I knew a man named Michael Finnegan, etc.

► Continue singing the song until you are ready to stop.

Adaptation

► Let the children make their own Michael Finnegan.

Take Your Little Hands

When?

Sing this song and use the body puppet to give directions or change activities.

Why?

The puppet encourages children to follow along and learn different parts of the body.

What?

paper grocery sack
construction paper scraps
crayons or markers
glue
scissors
stapler
yarn or string
old socks or hose (4)

Preparation

▶ Use the folded bottom of the sack as the head, and decorate it to look like an animal or person.

▶ Cut out hands and feet and staple them to the ends of the socks or hose. Staple these to the body to make arms and legs.

▶ Attach string or yarn to the top of the head, then hang it around your neck.

How?

▶ Move the puppet's arms while singing the following to the tune of "The Wheels on the Bus."

You take your little hands and go
Clap, clap, clap. Clap, clap, clap.
Clap, clap, clap.
You take your little hands and go
Clap, clap, clap. Clap, clap, clap.
Clap, clap, clap.

You take your little eyes and go
Blink, blink, blink...
You take your little lips and go
Kiss, kiss, kiss...
You take your little feet and go
Stomp, stomp, stomp...

Adaptations

▶ Make up other verses and motions, asking the children to clean up, sit down to eat, etc.

▶ Give the children different directions to follow using the body puppet, for example, touch his hand to his ear, touch his foot to his nose, etc.

▶ Let the children make their own body puppets for acting out stories and songs.

 PUPPET SONGS

Baby Bumblebee

When?

Focus children's attention with this song and the puppets.

Why?

The puppets prompt children to sing the various verses of the song.

What?

popsicle sticks
glue
scissors
markers
animal pictures, drawn or cut from magazines

Preparation

▶ Draw, color and cut out the animals shown.

▶ Glue them to the popsicle sticks.

How?

▶ Hold up the puppets one at a time while chanting the following.

I'm bringing home a baby bumblebee. (cup hands as if holding a bee)
Won't my mommy be so proud of me?
I'm bringing home a baby bumblebee.
Buzzy-wuzzy-buzzy-wuzzy. Oh, he stung me!

I'm bringing home a little baby bear.
Won't my mommy climb up in a chair?
I'm bringing home a little baby bear.
Growl, growl, growl, growl, growl. (hold up hands and growl)

I'm bringing home a little rattle snake.
Won't my mommy shiver and shake?
I'm bringing home a little rattle snake.
Sss, sss, sss, sss, sss. (move arm like a snake)

I'm bringing home a little baby skunk.
Won't my mommy throw it in a trunk?
I'm bringing home a little baby skunk.
Pew, pew, pew, pew, pew! (hold nose)

I'm bringing home a hippopotamus.
Won't my mommy raise a great big fuss?
I'm bringing home a hippopotamus.
Stomp, stomp, stomp, stomp, stomp. (stomp feet)

Adaptation

▶ Make up your own silly verses and appropriate puppets for this song.

QUIET SONGS

The Hug Song

When?

Get children's attention or get them back in their seats with this tune.

Why?

Children can always use words of encouragement.

What?

No materials are needed.

How?

► Model the words and motions for the children. They can follow along to the tune of "Row, Row, Row Your Boat."

Clap, clap, clap your hands. (clap hands)
Stomp, stomp, stomp your feet. (stomp feet)
Give yourself a great big hug. (mmmm)
    (hug self)
Because you are so neat.
Clap, clap, clap your hands. (clap hands)
Stomp, stomp, stomp your feet. (stomp feet)
Give yourself a great big hug. (mmmm)
    (hug self)
And then you take a seat.

Adaptation

► Ask the children why they're "neat" or why they like themselves.

 QUIET SONGS

My Pigeons

When?

Quiet the children for a story or another activity with this charming song.

Why?

Children will be fascinated by the finger pigeons and will want to imitate the movements.

What?

No materials are needed.

How?

- Make two fists.
- Put them next to each other.
- Stick up thumbs to make a pigeon house.

- Hold it close to your chest while chanting softly.

   My pigeon house I open wide
   (slowly open fingers)
   And set my pigeons free.
   (fly fingers in the air)
   They fly around on every side
   (fly fingers to the side)
   And in the highest tree.
   (fly fingers above your head)
   Then they come down at evening.
   (slowly bring hands back together)
   They close their eyes and sing.
   (make a pigeon house again)
   Coo roo, coo roo.
   (softly coo)
   Listen to them sing.

Adaptation

- Let the children act out the end of this chant by quietly sitting on the floor with their heads bowed and arms over their heads.

Twink a Link

When?

This is a peaceful song to sing to quiet children.

Why?

Children enjoy the words and the motions.

What?

No materials are needed.

How?

▶ Ask the children to make "stars" by holding their hands in the air as they open and close their fingers.

▶ Sing the following to the tune of "The Wheels on the Bus."

The stars at night go twink a link, (open and close hands)
Twink a link, twink a link.
The stars at night go twink a link
Oh, way up in the sky. (point to sky)

The moon at night goes blink a link, (blink eyes)
Blink a link, blink a link.
The moon at night goes blink a link
And shines right in my eyes. (point to eyes)

The skunk at night goes stink a link, (hold nose)
Stink a link, stink a link.
The skunk at night goes stink a link.
I wish he'd go right by.

▶ End the song by saying

Twink a link a link. (open and close hands)
Blink a link a link. (blink eyes)
Stink a link a link. (hold nose)
Oh, my! (wave hand in front of you)

Adaptation

▶ Make a big book of this song by writing the words and illustrating each verse on a separate page. Use poster board or heavy paper and fasten together with book rings.

  WAITING SONGS

B-I-N-G-O

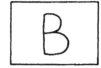   *front of cards*

    *back of cards*

When?

Bingo will entertain children of all ages during those in-between times.

Why?

Letters, sequencing and counting skills are reinforced by adding a prop to this familiar song.

What?

poster board
scissors
markers

Preparation

► Cut the poster board into five rectangles 8-1/2" x 11".

► On the front of each card print the letters, B, I, N, G, O.

► Number the cards on the back from 1-5 and draw a picture of hands clapping beneath the number.

How?

► Pass out the cards to five children.

► Have them stand up in front of the room in order from left to right.

► After each verse is sung, one card is turned over revealing a pair of clapping hands to indicate where to clap as the song continues.

There was a farmer had a dog
And Bingo was his name-o.
B-I-N-G-O, B-I-N-G-O, B-I-N-G-O,
And Bingo was his name-o.

► When the second verse is sung, clap instead of saying the letter B.

► For the third verse, clap for B and I.

► Continue leaving out letters and replacing them with a clap until you are clapping for all the letters.

Adaptations

► Change the words to introduce other letters of the alphabet. For example, "There was a frog who liked to hop and Jumpy was his name-o. J-U-M-P-Y, etc."

► Help children spell their names by singing them to this tune. "There is a boy that you all know and Derik is his name-o. D-E-R-I-K, etc."

 WAITING SONGS

Lollipops

When?

Use Lollipops while waiting for children to clean up, wash hands or between activities.

Why?

Singing makes everyone feel good, while enhancing language, auditory memory and motor skills. These Lollipops also encourage children to use pictures as clues and to associate print with the song titles.

What?

poster board scraps (different colors)
markers
scissors
popsicle sticks
cup or can
glue or tape

Preparation

➤ Cut 3" circles from the poster board.

➤ Write the titles of the class's favorite songs, chants or finger plays on the circles. Draw a picture related to the song.

➤ Glue or tape the circles to popsicle sticks to make lollipops and store in a can or cup.

How?

➤ When there are a few extra minutes, choose a child to pull out a lollipop.

➤ Sing or say that song, finger play or chant.

Adaptations

➤ Play "Name that Tune." Let one child hum a tune for the other children to guess.

➤ Older children could make and illustrate their own lollipops.

▶▶▶▶▶▶▶ 10 ▶▶▶▶▶▶▶

FINGER PLAYS AND CHANTS

Fingers that wiggle, dance and turn into hot dogs, caterpillars and other magical things fascinate children. As children quiet down and join in with finger plays, they are promoting language and motor skills and developing auditory memory. Use the rhymes in this chapter to gather children for group activities or to entertain them while they wait. They are an excellent indirect way to get children's attention.

Chants are another technique that can be used to focus children's attention and make them giggle. The rhymes, beats, motions and nonsense words will provide a positive, successful experience for all.

So clap, stomp,
Wiggle and dance.
Your class will enjoy
These poems and chants!

 **FINGER PLAYS**

The Apple Tree

  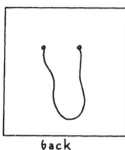 

back   front

When?

Children are fascinated by the moveable prop which accompanies this finger play.

Why?

Colors and numbers are reinforced in a meaningful way.

What?

poster board (12" x 16")
red construction paper
yarn
scissors
glue
tape
markers

Preparation

▶ Draw and color a large tree on the poster board.

▶ Cut two red apples from the construction paper.

▶ Poke two holes in the tree, then thread a piece of yarn 16" long from the back through the holes.

▶ Tape an apple to the end of each piece of yarn, then pull the yarn through to the back of the poster board so it looks like the apples are hanging on the tree.

How?

▶ While saying the following rhyme, pull on the apples to make them fall when you get to the appropriate line.

Way up high (point up)
In the apple tree.
Two little apples (hold up two fingers)
Smiled down at me. (look down and smile)
I shook that tree (pretend to shake a tree)
As hard as I could.
And down came the apples. (bring apples down)
MMMM! MMMM! GOOD! (pat tummy)

Adaptation

▶ Add the following verses to the rhyme.

Way up in the orange tree, one little orange, etc. . .
Way up in the lemon tree, one little lemon, etc. . .
Way up in the plum tree, one little plum, etc. . .
Way up in the lime tree, one little lime, etc. . .

 ▶▶▶▶▶▶ FINGER PLAYS ▶▶▶▶▶▶

The Caterpillar

When?

Quiet the children for a story or group activity with this poem.

Why?

The metamorphosis of a caterpillar into a butterfly is introduced with this finger play.

What?

No materials are needed.

How?

▶ Hold up an index finger.

▶ Wiggle it while saying, "Show me your caterpillar."

▶ Begin the rhyme.

> A caterpillar crawled (hold left hand in air and slowly wiggle right index finger up)
> To the top of a tree.
> "I think I'll take a nap,"
> Said he.
> So under a leaf (crawl right index finger to palm of left hand)
> He began to creep.
> He spun a cocoon
> And he fell asleep.

> For six long months
> He slept in that cocoon bed.
> Till spring came along
> And said, "Wake up. (shake hand)
> Wake up, you sleepy head."
> Out of the leaf (clasp thumbs together and flutter fingers like a butterfly)
> He began to creep.
> And he did cry,
> "Lo, I am a butterfly!"

Adaptation

▶ With an old sock, some pompoms and felt, make a magic caterpillar. On the outside of the sock, glue three pompoms to look like eyes and a mouth. Turn the sock inside out and sew a felt butterfly on the inside. To start the poem, show the sock caterpillar, pull the top of the sock over the toe and dangle it to look like the cocoon (or chrysalis), then poke the inside out to reveal the butterfly at the end.

▶▶▶▶▶▶ FINGER PLAYS ▶▶▶▶▶▶

Here's a Box

When?

Here's a box of surprises to get children interested in a story or group activity.

Why?

Creativity, language and dramatization are encouraged with this rhyme.

What?

No materials are needed.

How?

▶ Say the following rhyme with the appropriate hand movements.

▶ Give children turns guessing what is in the box.

Here's a box (form fist with left hand)
And here's the lid. (open right hand and
*   place on left fist)*
I wonder what
Inside is hid?

▶ Choose a child who names an animal or other object.

Yes, you're right, (smile and nod head)
Without a doubt.
Let's open the box (lift right hand)
And take it out.

▶ Pretend to take out whatever the child said and make a noise or motion to dramatize it.

Adaptations

▶ Let children stand up and move around the classroom and act out what is suggested to be in the box.

▶ Use a small gift box as a prop.

One Small Noodle

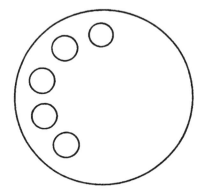
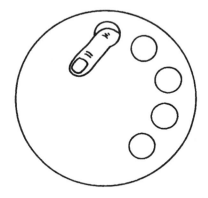

When?

This finger play can be used to focus children's attention for a story or group activity.

Why?

Children will enjoy using the prop as they learn the numbers one through five.

What?

paper plate
scissors

Preparation

▶ Draw five circles the size of your finger on the plate.

▶ Cut out the circles to make holes.

How?

▶ Put one finger in a hole.

▶ Wiggle it and begin the poem.

One small noodle (wiggle finger)
On my noodle plate.
Salt and pepper, (pretend to sprinkle salt
*   and pepper with other hand)*
Taste just great.
Mother's going
To the store.
Mother, mother,
Get some more.

Two small noodles... (stick in second finger)
Three small noodles... (stick in third finger)
Four small noodles... (stick in fourth finger)
Five small noodles... (stick in fifth finger)
Mother, mother, (shake head no)
I don't need more.

Adaptation

▶ Let children make their own plates and stick their fingers through as they say the rhyme. Color the plates and glue yarn on them for noodles.

 FINGER PLAYS

Five Monkeys Swinging From a Tree

When?

As children gather for a story or circle time, use this finger play to settle them down.

Why?

Numbers and subtraction are introduced as the little monkeys disappear.

What?

No materials are needed.

How?

▶ Hold up five fingers, then begin the rhyme.

Five little monkeys, (hold up five fingers)
Hanging from a tree. (wiggle fingers)
Teasing Mr. Alligator, (point with finger as
   you say this)
"Can't catch me.
You can't catch me."
Along comes Mr. Alligator (say slowly;
   make alligator mouth by putting two
   hands together)
Quiet as can be,
And snatched one monkey
Right out of the tree! (clap hands on
   snatched)

Four little monkeys...
Three little monkeys...
Two little monkeys...
One little monkey...

No little monkeys
Hanging from a tree.
Teasing Mr. Alligator,
"Can't catch me.
You can't catch me."
Along comes Mr. Alligator
Quiet as can be,
"I'm full,"
Said he.

Adaptation

▶ Let the children act out being the little monkeys and the alligator.

 FINGER PLAYS

Five Monkeys Jumping on the Bed

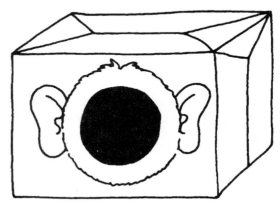

When?

Here are more silly monkeys to entertain children for a few minutes.

Why?

Children enjoy being the monkeys, and they develop number concepts.

What?

5 large brown paper grocery sacks
markers or crayons
scissors

Preparation

▶ Cut off 7" from the top of the bags.

▶ On one side of each bag cut out a 6-1/2" circle.

▶ Draw a monkey's face around the circles as shown and color them in.

How?

▶ Select five children to put on the monkey masks.

▶ They pretend that they are monkeys jumping on a bed as the rest of the group says the finger play.

Five little monkeys
Jumping on the bed.
One fell off
And bumped his head.
Momma called the doctor
And the doctor said,
"That's what you get
For jumping on the bed."

Four little monkeys...
Three little monkeys...
Two little monkeys...
One little monkey...

▶ At the end of each verse one monkey sits down.

Adaptation

▶ Change the words to "Five little mommies jumping on the bed," or "Five little bunnies jumping on the bed," or use other characters and animals.

 FINGER PLAYS

Elephants

1. Cut a hole in plate.
2. Paint grey.
3. Add eyes and mouth.
4. trace hands & cut out
   grey paper
5. attach "ears"
6. pull sock over hand
7. put hand & sock through hole
Grey

When?

Give children something interesting to look at with the visual for this poem.

Why?

Children want to listen to what the elephant has to say.

What?

paper plate
crayons or markers
gray construction paper
scissors
glue
old white sock
2 brad fasteners

Preparation

▶ Cut a hole in the middle of the plate approximately 2-1/2" wide. (It needs to be big enough for your hand to go through.)

▶ Color the plate gray and add eyes and a mouth.

▶ To make elephant ears, trace around your hands on the gray construction paper and attach them to the plate with the brads.

▶ Put the sock on your hand, then stick it through the hole to look like the elephant's trunk.

How?

▶ Wiggle the elephant's trunk, then repeat this poem.

Elephants walk (sway from side to side)
Like this and that.
They're terribly big (spread arms wide)
And terribly fat.
They have no hands. (hold up hands)
They have no toes. (point to toes)
But goodness, gracious, (extend arms in front of you to look like a trunk)
What a nose!

▶ Tell the children to put on their elephant ears to listen to directions, a story, etc.

Adaptation

▶ Give children the opportunity to make their own elephant puppets from paper plates.

▶▶▶▶▶▶ FINGER PLAYS ▶▶▶▶▶▶

Five Little Hot Dogs

When?

Use this finger play mitt to focus children's attention while waiting for lunch or settling down for a story.

Why?

This finger play promotes the development of language, math concepts and a longer attention span.

What?

cloth work glove
velcro
red and brown felt scraps
10 wiggly eyes
fabric glue
scissors
felt pen

Preparation

▶ Cut the velcro into five 1" strips. Glue or sew the fuzzy side of the velcro to the palm side of each finger on the glove.

▶ Using the pattern shown on the next page, cut out five hot dogs and five buns. Glue the hot dogs to the buns.

▶ Decorate the hot dogs with wiggly eyes and a felt pen.

▶ Glue the loop side of the velcro to the back of each hot dog.

▶ Store in a ziplock bag along with the words to the finger play.

How?

▶ Put the hot dogs on all five fingers of the mitt.

▶ Keep the mitt in a pocket or other handy place.

▶ Ask the children to hold up five fingers.

▶ Put on the mitt and say the following.

Five little hot dogs frying in the pan. (hold up five fingers)
The grease got hot and one went BAM! (clap hands on BAM! and remove a hot dog)

Four little hot dogs... (hold up four fingers; clap and remove another hot dog on BAM!)
Three little hot dogs...
Two little hot dogs...
One little hot dog...
No little hot dogs frying in the pan.
The pan got hot and it went BAM!

Adaptations

▶ Write the words to the finger play on a language experience chart.

▶ Let the children stand up and act out the rhyme, sitting down when each hot dog goes BAM!

▶ Use the mitt (with doughnuts attached) for the following finger play, sung to the tune of "Five Little Ducks That I Once Knew."

Five little doughnuts in a bakery shop,
Round and fat with sugar on top.
Along came (child's name) with a penny one
*   day.*
She bought a doughnut and she took it away.

Four little doughnuts...

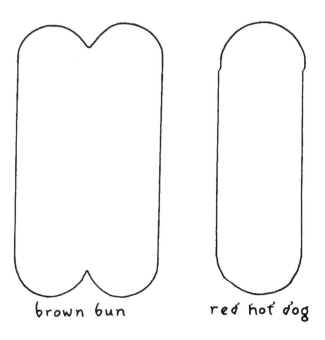

brown bun   red hot dog

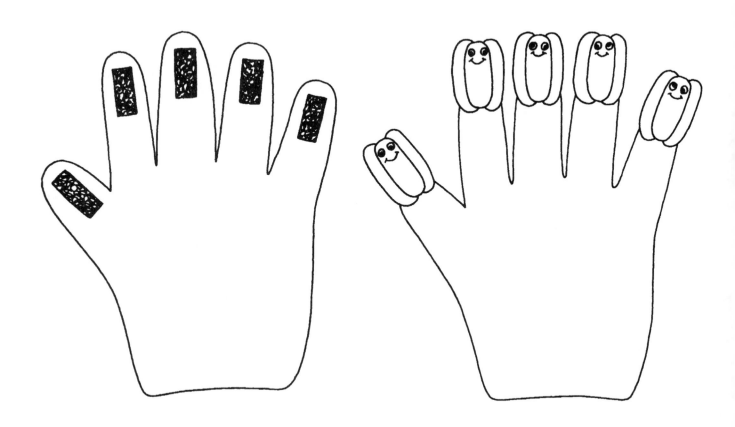

 FINGER PLAYS

Seasonal Rhymes

When?

Celebrate special times of the year with these finger plays.

Why?

Language skills and auditory memory are developed as children say these rhymes.

What?

You may want to make felt flannel board pieces or stick puppets of the characters for each poem.

How?

➤ Choose a finger play for the appropriate time of year.

Spring

"Five Little Kites"

1, 2, 3, 4, 5 little kites,
Flying up in the sky
Said "Hi" to the clouds as they passed by.
Said "Hi" to the birds,
Said "Hi" to the sun.
Said "Hi" to the airplanes, Oh, what fun!
Then, swish, went the wind,
And they all took a dive.
1, 2, 3, 4, 5.

"Five Little Birdies"

Five little birds sitting on my door.
One jumped off, then there were four.
Four little birds happy as can be.
One flew away, and then there were three.
Three little birds with nothing to do.
One fell off, then there were two.
Two little birds chirping in the sun.
A bird flew away, then there was one.
One little bird sitting in the sun.
Away he flew, and there were none.

"Hippity-Hop Bunnies"

Hippity-hop and hippity-hay,
Five little bunnies went out to play.
Hippity-hop and hippity-hay,
One little bunny runs away.

Hippity-hop and hippity-hay, four...
Hippity-hop and hippity-hay, three...
Hippity-hop and hippity-hay, two...
Hippity-hop and hippity-hay, one...
Hippity-hop and hippity-hay, where did all
the bunnies go?

Summer

"Five Little Fishes"

Five little fishes swimming in the pool.
First one said, "The pool is cool."
Second one said, "The pool is deep."
Third one said, "I want to sleep."
Fourth one said, "Let's dive and dip."
Fifth one said, "I spy a ship."

The fishermen came and their lines went ker-splash,
And away those five little fishies did dash!

"Five Little Seashells"

Five little seashells lying on the shore.
Swish, went the waves, and then there were four.
Four little seashells, cozy as could be.
Swish, went the waves, and then there were three.
Three little seashells, all pearly new.
Swish, went the waves and then there were two.
Two little seashells, sleeping in the sun.
Swish, went the waves, and then there was one.
One little seashell left all alone.
It whispered, "Shhhh," as I took it home.

Fall

"Five Pumpkins"

Five little pumpkins sitting on a gate.
The first one said, "Oh, my, it's getting late."
The second one said, "There are witches in the air."
The third one said, "But we don't care."
The fourth one said, "Let's run and run and run."
The fifth one said, "I'm ready for some fun."
Then "whoooo" went the wind, and out went the lights,
And the five little pumpkins rolled out of sight.

"Five Turkeys"

Five little turkeys were standing by my door.
One saw some corn, and then there were four.
Four little turkeys up in a tree.
One fell down and then there were three.
Three little turkeys gobbled as they do.
A dog chased one, and then there were two.
Two little turkeys strutting in the sun.
The wind came along, and then there was one.
One little turkey and he flew far away.
He knew it was close to Thanksgiving Day!

Winter

"Five Little Bells"

Five little bells ring with a chime,
To tell of happy holiday time.
Four little bells ring sweet and clear,
To tell that Christmas Day is here.
Three little bells ring soft and low,
To tell of stockings in a row.
Two little bells ring merrily,
To tell of toys beneath the tree.
One little bell rings silver bright,
To welcome Santa Claus tonight.

"Snowmen"

Five little snowmen
With buttons from the store.
This one melted,
And then there were four.
Four little snowmen beneath a pine tree.
This one melted,
And then there were three.
Three little snowmen
Glad that they know you.
This one melted
And then there were two.
Two little snowmen
Playing and having fun.
This one melted
And then there was one.
One little snowman
Left all alone.
He melted all away,
And then there was none.

"Five Red Valentines"

Five red valentines from the ten cent store.
I sent one to mother, and now there are four.
Four red valentines, pretty ones to see.
I gave one to brother, so now there are three.
Three red valentines that say I love you.
I gave one to sister, and now there are two.
Two red valentines, my, we have fun.
I gave one to daddy, and now there is one.
One red valentine and the story is almost done.
I gave it to baby, and now there is none.

CHANTS

Nursery Rhyme Rock

When?

As children wait in line or at in-between times, this nursery rhyme rap will keep them from getting restless.

Why?

This activity adds a modern twist to some old rhymes.

What?

No materials are needed.

How?

► Stand or sit.

► Clap and snap to get a rhythm going.

Chorus:
   *Humpty Dumpty. (clap, snap, clap, snap to
      the rhythm of the words)*
   Hump-Dump-de-Dumpty.
   Humpty Dumpty.
   Hump-Dump-de-Dumpty.

   Little Miss Muffet (slap legs)
   Sat on her tuffet
   Eating her curds and whey.
   Along came a spider
   Who sat down beside her.
   And he said,
   *"Oh, that's so funny now!" (snap one finger
      in the air)*

Humpty Dumpty Chorus

Little boy blue (slap legs)
Come blow your horn.
The sheep's in the meadow.
The cow's in the corn.
Where is that boy
Who looks after the sheep?
He's under the haystack saying,
*"Oh, that's so funny now!" (snap one finger
   in the air)*

Humpty Dumpty Chorus

► Continue adding other nursery rhymes and changing the last line to, "Oh, that's so funny now" or any other phrase.

► End with the Humpty Dumpty chorus, said gradually more softly until it is just a whisper.

Dr. Knicker Bocker

When?

Get rid of wiggles and squirms with this active chant.

Why?

Dr. Knicker Bocker helps the children develop large muscles, coordination and sequencing skills.

What?

No materials are needed.

How?

▶ Have the children stand up and begin slapping their thighs and snapping their fingers.

▶ When everyone has the rhythm, begin the following chant.

Dr. Knicker Bocker
Knicker Bocker
Number nine.
We can get the rhythm
Most any old time.

Who can get the rhythm
In their hands? Clap, clap. (clap hands twice)
Oh, we can get the rhythm
In our hands. Clap, clap. (clap twice)

Who can get the rhythm
In their feet? Stomp, stomp. (stomp feet twice)
Oh, we can get the rhythm
In our feet. Stomp, stomp. (stomp twice)

Who can get the rhythm
In their heads? Ding, dong... (move head from side to side)

Who can get the rhythm
In their hips? Hot dog... (put hands on hips and wiggle)

Who can get the rhythm
In their arms? Whoopee! (raise arms and shout, "whoopee!")
Who can get the rhythm
All over? Clap, clap, (put all the previous motions together)
Stomp, stomp,
Ding dong,
Hot dog,
Whoopee!

Adaptation

▶ For little ones who can't snap, simply slap thighs and clap hands to the rhythm.

▶▶▶▶▶▶ CHANTS ▶▶▶▶▶▶

Boom Chica Boom

When?

This chant can be used while waiting for a new activity to begin. Keep adding verses if needed.

Why?

What a silly way to dramatize and practice language skills!

What?

No materials are needed.

How?

▶ Tell the children this is an echo chant.

▶ They repeat each line.

I said a boom chica boom. (children repeat)
I said a boom chica boom. (children repeat)
I said a boom chica rocka chica rocka chica boom. (children repeat)
Un, huh. (children repeat)
Oh, yeah. (children repeat)
One more time. (children repeat)

▶ Try one of the following versions.

▶ Opera version—Sing the verses, using arms and a dramatic voice.

▶ Grumpy version—Put a frown on your face and stomp your feet.

▶ Underwater version—Put your forefinger between your lips and move up and down.

Adaptations

▶ End this chant with a silent version. Mouth the words without any sound.

▶ Make up your own funny versions.

CHANTS

Hicklety Picklety Bumblebee

When?

Use this chant to gather children for a group activity or keep their interest as they wait for others.

Why?

Children enjoy hearing their names said as they join the rhythm.

What?

No materials are needed.

How?

➤ Slap thighs and snap fingers, then go around the circle using each child's name in this chant.

Hicklety picklety bumblebee! (slap and snap to the beat)
Who can say their name for me?
(Child's name) (point to a child)
Repeat child's name.
Clap it.
(Child's name) (clap as you say it)
Whisper it.
(Child's name) (whisper child's name)
No sound.
(Child's name) (mouth child's name)

➤ Continue using other children's names.

Adaptations

➤ If the children can't snap fingers, then just clap to the beat.

➤ After each child hears his name, he goes to another activity.

➤ "Shakey, Shakey" will also entertain children as they wait.

(Name), (Name) sick in bed.
Called the doctor and the doctor said,
"Come on, (name), you're not sick,
All you need is an exercise trick."
So stand up and shakey, shakey, shakey
(child stands and shakes hands in the air).
Get down and shakey, shakey, shakey
*   (shakes hands low).*
Turn around and shakey, shakey, shakey
*   (shakes hands while turning around).*
Turn around and shakey, shakey, shakey
*   (shakes hands while turning around).*
Sit down and shakey, shakey, shakey (Child
*   sit back down).*

CHANTS

Hi, My Name Is Joe

When?

If children are tense and restless, shake it out with this movement game.

Why?

Learn left and right and parts of the body in a fun way.

What?

No materials are needed.

How?

▶ Have the children stand.

▶ Ask them to follow the motions to the chant.

> *Hi, my name is Joe.*
> *I've got a wife and three kids*
> *And I work in a button factory.*
> *One day, my boss came to me*
> *And said, "Joe, are you busy?"*
> *I said, "No."*
> *"Then work with your right hand." (start moving your right hand up and down)*

▶ Second verse—Say the first six lines, ending with,

> *"Then work with your left hand." (move left hand along with right)*

▶ Third verse—Say the first six lines, ending with,

> *"Then work with your right foot." (move both hands and right foot)*

▶ Fourth verse—Say the first six lines, ending with,

> *"Then work with your left foot." (move both hands and feet)*

▶ Fifth verse—Say the first six lines, ending with,

> *"Then work with your head." (move hands, feet and head up and down)*

▶ Final verse—Say the first four lines and after, "Joe, are you busy?"

> *I said, "Yes!" (shout out the last line)*

Adaptations

▶ Try this silly verse. "Then work your tongue." (move tongue back and forth in mouth while trying to talk)

▶ Write the letter "L" on the child's left hand and the letter "R" on her right hand with a washable marker to help her learn left and right.

 CHANTS ▶▶▶▶▶▶▶

The Frog Chant

When?

Pick up children's attention or spirits with this chant.

Why?

Repetition fosters auditory memory and language.

What?

No materials are needed.

How?

▶ Explain that this is an echo chant, so the children will have to listen carefully to repeat what is said.

Dog.
Dog-cat.
Dog-cat-fish.
Dog-cat-fish-bird.
Itsy bitsy teeny weeny little green froggie.
Jump high, catch a fly, little green froggie.
Spiders and worms are scrumpdilly-icious.
Ribbit, ribbit, ribbit, ribbit, ribbit, ribbit,
   Croak!

Adaptation

▶ Slap thighs and clap hands to the rhythm of this chant.

▶▶▶▶▶▶ CHANTS ▶▶▶▶▶▶

Dum Dum Da Da

When?

To gather children for a group activity, just begin this chant and continue it until everyone has joined the group.

Why?

Children develop motor skills and coordination as they follow along.

What?

No materials are needed.

How?

▶ Sit on the floor, put hands on thighs and begin.

Dum dum da da, (pat thighs to the rhythm)
Dum dum da da,
Dum dum da da da,
Dum dum dum da da,
Dum dum da da,
Dum dum da da da dum.

▶ Second Verse: Clap and snap the beat.

▶ Third Verse: Roll hands.

▶ Fourth Verse: Wave hands over each other.

▶ Continue doing other hand motions until everyone is sitting down.

Adaptation

▶ Let the children suggest different motions.

CHANTS

Oliver Twist

When?

Entertain children while they are waiting or use this chant for a break between activities.

Why?

Children learn to cooperate with a partner.

What?

No materials are needed.

How?

► Have children stand and put their hands on their hips as they follow along.

Oliver Twist, Twist, Twist, (twist from side to side)
Can't do this, this, this. (twist)
Touch your hair, hair, hair. (touch your hair)
Touch your toes, toes, toes. (touch your toes)
Touch your back, back, back. (touch your back)
Touch your nose, nose, nose. (touch your nose)

► Face a partner and say the rhyme, touching his hair, toes, back and nose.

► Stand side by side with a partner and say the rhyme, touching her hair, toes, back and nose.

► Stand back to back with a partner and say the rhyme, trying to touch his hair, toes, back and nose.

► Return to the original position and say the rhyme a final time touching your own hair, toes, back and nose.

 CHANTS ▶▶▶▶▶▶▶

Silly Willy

When?

Shake those sillies out with Silly Willy.

Why?

As children move and develop coordination, they are learning to identify parts of the body and to tell right and left.

What?

No materials are needed.

How?

▶ Tell the children Silly Willy wants to meet them.

▶ Ask them to stand and follow along.

I know a little boy. (dance from side to side as you clap)
Yeah!
His name is Silly Willy.
Yeah!
He is so very nice,
But, oh, he acts so silly.
And so goes his right hand, (move right hand in and out)
And his right hand goes like so,
And his right hand is always soooo.

I know a little boy. (dance from side to side as you clap)
Yeah!
His name is Silly Willy.
Yeah!
He is so very nice,
But, oh, he acts so silly.
And so goes his left hand, (move left hand, then move right hand)
And his left hand goes like so,
And his left hand is always soooo.
And so goes his right hand,
And his right hand goes like so,
And his right hand is always soooo.

▶ Continue with additional verses, adding the right foot, left foot, shoulders and head.

▶▶▶▶▶▶ CHANTS ▶▶▶▶▶▶

Who Took the Cookie?

When?

While waiting for children to join the group, while riding on the bus or dealing with a little crisis, involve the children with this chant.

Why?

Social skills are encouraged as children call on friends and say each other's names.

What?

No materials are needed.

How?

▶ Sit down.

▶ Ask the children to follow along with the beat and words.

Who took the cookie (clap and snap)
From the cookie jar?
(Child's name) took the cookie
From the cookie jar.
Who me? (child answers)
Yes, you. (group says)
Couldn't be. (child responds)
Then who? (group asks)
(Second child). (first child names a friend)

(Second child) took the cookie
From the cookie jar.
Who me? (second child answers)
Yes, you. (group says)
Couldn't be. (second child responds)
Then who? (group asks)
(Third child). (second child names another
friend)

▶ The game continues as the children call on each other.

▶ The last child ends the game by responding "possibly" instead of "couldn't be."

Adaptations

▶ Each child goes to another activity after his name is used.

▶ Use this chant on a day when you have real cookies for snack.

CHANTS

Did You Ever, Ever, Ever?

When?

Try this chant to extend a group activity or get children's attention.

Why?

Encourages creativity in children.

What?

No materials are needed.

How?

➤ Slap thighs and clap hands to the rhythm of this chant.

Did you ever, ever, ever?
  (clap and snap to the beat)
Did you ever, ever, ever?
See a cow take a bow?
Oh, no! (put hands up in the air, then bring
  them down as you pretend to laugh)
Did you ever, ever, ever
See a dog kiss a frog?
Oh, no!
Did you ever, ever, ever
See a pig dance a jig?
Oh, no!

Did you ever, ever, ever
See a goat wear a coat?
Oh, no!
Did you ever, ever, ever
See a snake in a cake?
Oh, no!
Did you ever, ever, ever
See a moose dance with a goose?
Oh, no!

➤ Encourage the children to make up their own silly verses.

Adaptation

➤ Make a big book to go along with the verses and let the children illustrate them.

 CHANTS

Head, Shoulders, Baby

When?

Here's a hand game that gives children the opportunity to move and interact with friends between activities.

Why?

Eye-hand coordination and cooperation are developed with this chant.

What?

No materials are needed.

How?

➤ Let each child find a partner.

➤ The partners face each other.

➤ Show the children how to play a simple hand game by clapping and slapping alternating palms.

➤ After they practice, try the chant below.

*Head, shoulders, (touch head, then
   shoulders)
Baby, (clap)
One, (slap right palms together)
Two, (clap, then slap left palms)
Three. (clap, then slap right palms again)*

*Head, shoulders, (touch head, then
   shoulders)
Baby, (clap)
One, (slap right palms together)
Two, (clap, then slap left palms)
Three. (clap, then slap right palms again)
Head, shoulders, (touch head, then
   shoulders)*

*Head, shoulders, (touch head, then
   shoulders)
Baby, (clap)
One, (slap right palms together)
Two, (clap, then slap left palms)
Three. (clap, then slap right palms again)*

*Shoulders, waist, baby...
Waist, knees, baby...
Knees, toes, baby...
That's all, baby, please sit down.*

▶▶▶▶▶▶   CHANTS   ▶▶▶▶▶▶

Three Short-Necked Buzzards

When?

Take a break or fill an in-between time with this action chant.

Why?

Sets of three are introduced in a fun way, and children love the exaggerated motions.

What?

No materials are needed.

How?

▶ Have children stand and follow along with the motions and words.

Three short-necked (hold up three fingers)
Buzzards (lift shoulders, bend elbows)
Three short-necked (hold up three fingers)
Buzzards (lift shoulders, bend elbows)
Three short-necked (hold up three fingers)
Buzzards (lift shoulders, bend elbows)
Sitting in a dead tree. (hold up hands like a dead tree)
One flew aaaway.
What aaaa shame! (bend and put hands on knees)

Two short-necked buzzards...

One short-necked buzzard...

No short-necked buzzards
No short-necked buzzards
No short-necked buzzards
Sitting in a dead tree. (hold up hands like a dead tree)
One came back.
Let's reejoice! (cheer with hands)

One short-necked buzzard...
Two short-necked buzzards...
Three short-necked buzzards...

▶▶▶▶▶▶ CHANTS ▶▶▶▶▶▶

Peanut Butter

When?

Release energy and build group spirits with this cheerful chant.

Why?

Sequencing skills are developed as children move to the rhythm.

What?

No materials are needed.

How?

▶ Children stand or sit as they join along.

Peanut butter chorus:

> Peanut, (shake hands to the right)
> Peanut butter, (shake hands to the left)
> And jelly. (say softly as you shake down)
> Peanut, (shake hands to the right)
> Peanut butter, (shake hands to the left)
> And jelly. (say softly as you shake down)

> First you take the peanuts (pretend to pick
>   peanuts in the air)
> And you pick 'em, you pick 'em,
> You pick 'em, pick 'em, pick 'em.
>   Chorus

> Then you take the peanuts (pretend to crush
>   with hands)
> And you crush 'em, you crush 'em,

> You crush 'em, crush 'em, crush 'em.
>   Chorus

> Then you take the bread (hold out one hand
>   and spread with other hand)
> And you spread 'em...
>   Chorus

> Then you take the grapes (pretend to pick
>   grapes)
> And you pick 'em...
>   Chorus

> Then you take the grapes (crush grapes)
> And you crush 'em...
>   Chorus

> Then you take the bread (spread grapes)
> And you spread 'em...
>   Chorus

> Then you take your sandwich (smash hands)
> And you smash it...

▶ Pretend to bite and chew, then mumble because your mouth gets stuck with the peanut butter, while chanting the following.

> Then you take your sandwich
> And you eat it, you mmmmmm.
> Mmmmmm, mmmmmm, mmmmmm.
> Mmmmmm, mmmmmm, mmmmmm
> Mmmmmm.

▶▶▶▶▶▶ 11 ▶▶▶▶▶▶

STORIES & LANGUAGE ACTIVITIES

One of the best transition activities is to tell children a story or read them a book. By using the imaginative tales in this chapter, the children will believe you are a storyteller, even if you don't consider yourself one. Stories foster key elements of language development, such as listening and comprehension skills and a longer attention span, in addition to giving a great deal of pleasure to children. The children will beg you to tell many of these stories again. And don't hesitate to make up your own stories such as adventures you had as a child. You may also discover that some of the children are enthusiastic about telling their own stories.

Big books, book buddies, coffee can theater, group stories and flannel board stories are just a few of the creative ideas that will integrate whole language and a love of reading and writing into transition times.

 STORIES

Mitch the Fish

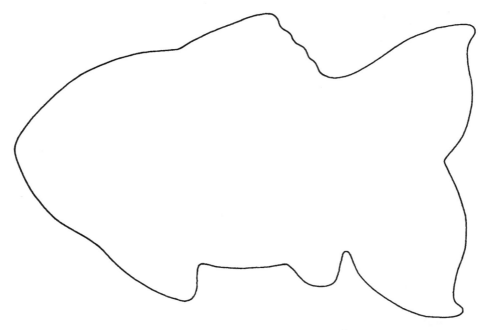

When?

"Mitch the Fish" entertains children. The story can be repeated many, many times.

Why?

Color identification skills are reinforced as Mitch changes his colors.

What?

letter-size file folder
scissors
tape
orange, red, yellow, blue and black con-
    struction paper
crayons or makers

Preparation

▶ Trace the fish shape (see illustration) on one side of the file folder and cut it out. Color around the fish so that it looks like the ocean.

▶ Tape the sides of the folder together.

▶ Cut the construction paper into 7" x 9" rectangles. (You will need two orange and one of each of the other colors.)

▶ Place the construction paper pieces into the file folder behind the fish cutout in this order: orange, red, yellow, blue, black and orange.

How?

▶ Tell the story of Mitch, removing one colored paper at a time from the file folder to make him a different color.

"Mitch the Fish"

Once there was an orange fish named Mitch who could change his color with the swish of his tail. All he had to say was,

> *"I'm Mitch the fish.*
> *I swim and I swish.*
> *And I can change my color*
> *If I wish."*

One day he was swimming around on the ocean floor and he saw a red lobster. He thought it would be fun to be a bright color like the lobster so he said,

> *"I'm Mitch the fish.*
> *I swim and I swish.*
> *And I can change my color*
> *If I wish."*

Suddenly he turned red. (Remove the orange sheet of paper to make Mitch red.) The lobster said, "Im the only sea creature who can be red. I'll snap at you!" So Mitch decided he didn't want to be red anymore. Just then he saw a yellow starfish, so he said,

> *"I'm Mitch the fish.*
> *I swim and I swish.*
> *And I can change my color*
> *If I wish."*

And with a swish Mitch turned yellow. (Remove the red paper to show the yellow.) The starfish said, "I'm the only creature who can be yellow. I'll prickle you!" So Mitch decided he didn't want to be yellow anymore. Mitch sees a blue whale and turns blue. The whale threatens to spout water on Mitch, so Mitch decides to turn black like the shark, but the shark says he will poke Mitch. Finally, Mitch says,

> *"I'm Mitch the fish.*
> *I swim and I swish.*
> *And I can change my color*
> *If I wish."*

So, Mitch changed back into being an orange fish again. Because being yourself is the very best thing you can be!

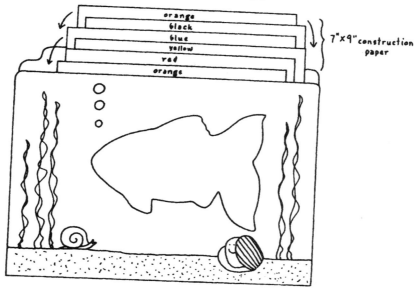

STORIES

Participation Story

When?

This story lets children get rid of their wiggles in a positive way.

Why?

Children develop listening skills as they respond to the story.

What?

No materials are needed.

How?

► Assign children to be the different characters below.

► Two or three children can be each character.

► Instruct them to stand up, turn around and sit back down whenever their name is said in the story.

► When telling the story, pause slightly after saying each character's name.

The Wiggle Family

Mama
Papa
Sister
Brother
Baby
Dog

Cat
House
Grandpa
Grandma
Van

One day Mama Wiggle said, "Why don't we all get in the van and take a trip to Grandma and Grandpa Wiggles' house." Papa got the van while Sister packed a lunch. Mother got the baby, and Brother got the cat and dog. Soon Mother, Father and Baby were in the front of the van, and Sister and Brother, the cat and the dog were in the back of the van.

"Oh, no," said Sister, "I forgot the picnic lunch! We'll never make it all the way to Grandma and Grandpa's house without something to eat."

So Mama told Papa to stop the van. They turned around and drove back to their house to get the picnic lunch. Sister ran back to the house while the others sat in the van. Just then the dog started barking and scared the cat who jumped out of the van. Brother had to chase the cat and bring her back to the van. The Baby got so upset he just cried and cried. Soon Mama, Papa, Sister, Brother, Baby, the dog and cat were all back in the van and were on their way to Grandma and Grandpa's house, and they all had a wonderful day.

Adaptation

► Make up your own silly versions of this story and other participation stories.

▶▶▶▶▶▶   STORIES   ▶▶▶▶▶▶

The Little Frog With the Big Mouth

When?

If a laugh is needed, or on a particularly noisy day, just remember this story about the little frog.

Why?

Children will be delighted by the lesson the little frog learns.

What?

No materials are needed.

How?

▶ Sit down with the children.

▶ Open your mouth as wide as you can.

▶ Tell the funny story about a little frog.

"Little Frog with the Big Mouth"

Once there was a little frog with a big mouth. One day he was catching flies and eating them with his mother when he asked,"Mama Frog, what do the other animals feed their babies?" (Whenever the little frog speaks, open your mouth wide and really draw out each word.)

"I don't know," Mama Frog answered. "Why don't we go ask them?"

Little Frog hopped along until he came to Mama Cow. "Mama Cow, what do you feed your baby cow?"

"I feed my baby cow hay," Mama Cow said.

"Oh, thank you," said the little frog, and he hopped until he came to Mama Pig. "Mama Pig, what do you feed your baby pig?"

"I feed my baby pig corn," replied Mama Pig.

"Oh, thank you," said the little frog as he hopped over to Mrs. Cat. "Mama Cat, what do you feed your baby kitten?"

"I feed my baby kitten milk," she answered.

"Oh, thank you," said the little frog, and he hopped down to the pond where Mama Alligator lived. "Mama Alligator, what do you feed your baby alligator?"

"I feed my baby alligator big mouth frogs," she replied.

"Oh, thank you," said the little frog and he quickly and quietly hopped home to his Mama. (Say this last line with your lips close together in a little voice.)

Adaptation

▶ Let the children act out or make puppets of this story.

Room for One More

When?

This is a good tale for a rainy day.

Why?

This story stresses the importance of sharing and good manners.

What?

an umbrella

How?

▶ Hold an umbrella, and each time a character joins the story, open up the umbrella a little bit.

▶ The umbrella should be fully open when the bear crawls in; then when the ant comes, quickly close the umbrella with a Pop!

"Room for One More"

Once there was a little mouse who lived in the forest. One day it started to rain, so he ran and hid under a mushroom, which made a perfect umbrella for a little mouse! Soon a frog hopped by.

"Say, may I please join you?" asked the frog politely.

"I suppose there's always room for one more," answered the mouse. So the mouse moved over
and made room for the frog. And the mushroom grew a little. Before long a little bird came along.*

"Please, do you think you could let me in under the mushroom? Im getting awfully wet out here," asked the little bird.

"Well, we'll squeeze in a little. There's always room for one more," replied the mouse.

When a rabbit hopped by and saw how cozy the other animals looked huddled together under the mushroom, he asked, "May I join you, please?"

"There's always room for one more," answered the mouse, as the mushroom grew even bigger. Next a fox came by.

"Im so wet and cold," said the fox. "May I please join you under the mushroom?"

"Always room for one more," said the mouse as the other animals squeezed in tighter.

"Please, please, may I come in from the rain with you?" begged a big bear that came along.

"Oh, dear," thought the mouse. "Well, there's always room for one more, I guess." The animals all huddled in closer and the mushroom grew as big as it could. Just then a little ant crawled by. Without so much as a "please" or "thank you" the little ant tried to join the others under the mushroom. That little ant just pushed and shoved until POP! The mushroom burst into a hundred pieces. And what do you think happened then? That's right! All the animals had to scurry and find another place to keep dry.

Something Special for You

When?

Here's the perfect story to tell before snack—especially if apples are on the menu.

Why?

There's a surprise at the end of this "tell and draw" story that all the children will enjoy.

What?

large sheet of paper and marker or chalk-board and chalk
grocery sack, apples, knife

How?

▶ Place the apples in the grocery sack, along with the knife.

▶ Draw the following illustrations on the paper or chalkboard as you tell the story.

"Something Special for You"

Once there was a little old lady who lived in the mountains in a little house right here. One day she decided to go down the mountain to town, so she left her house and started down the road like this.

On the way she met (child's name), and he asked, "Where are you going on such a fine day?" "I'm going down to town," replied the little old lady. "What are you going to get?" asked (child's name). "You'll just have to wait and see," said the lady.

On she walked until she met (child's name) and (child's name), and the other boys and girls. They all asked her, "Where are you going on such a fine day?"

"I'm going down to town," she replied. "What are you going to get?" they asked. "You'll just have to wait and see," the lady told them. The little old lady finally got to town. She went in the store and she came out with a big bag. *(At this point, take out the bag and hold it up.)*

She started back up the mountain like this, when all the boys and girls came running up to her. "What did you get? What's in your bag?" they all begged. "I've got some stars," the little old lady answered. "Come home with me and I'll give you each one."

So the little old lady and all the boys and girls continued up the mountain like this. They finally reached her house, and she opened her bag and pulled out an apple. *(Open the bag and take out an apple and the knife.)*

"But where are the stars?" questioned the children. The little old lady took the knife, cut the apple in half, and showed the children a beautiful star inside the apple. *(Cut the apple in half horizontally and show the children the star.)* Then she cut all the apples in half and gave all the children a star of their very own!

Adaptation

▶ Talk about how the children are like apples. They are all different on the outside, but there's a special star in each of them. Encourage them to share what's special about them on the inside.

▶▶▶▶▶▶ STORIES ▶▶▶▶▶▶

The Muffin Man

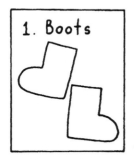 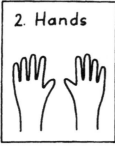  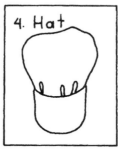 

When?

Ask the Muffin Man to visit the class when children are waiting for a new activity to begin.

Why?

Children read pictures before they read words, so the posters for this action story develop reading readiness and sequencing skills.

What?

poster board
scissors
markers

Preparation

▶ Cut the poster board into five sheets that are 10" x 12".

▶ Draw one of the following on the cards: Boots, Hands, Apron, Hat, Face

How?

▶ Choose five children to come to the front of the room and hold the poster cards.

▶ They should hold their cards facing them so no one sees it until the appropriate place in the story.

"The Muffin Man"

There was once an old lady who lived far out in the country all by herself. Every day she would just sit there and rock and spin all day long.

One day she heard a knock at the door. She called, "Come in," and in came a pair of boots. (Have the child holding the picture of the boots turn it over.) "I can't talk to old boots," said the lady, so she just continued to rock and spin.

A little later on there was another knock at the door. She called, "Come in," and in came two big hands. (Turn over the picture of the hands.) "I can't talk to hands," said the lady, so she just continued to rock and spin.

Soon there was another knock at the door. "Come in," called the lady and in came a big apron. (Turn over the card with the apron.) "I can't talk

to a big apron," said the little old lady, so she just kept on rocking and spinning.

She heard another knock at her door, and she called, "Come in." This time a big hat came in. (Turn over the picture of the hat.) "I can't talk to an old hat," she said, so she continued to rock and spin.

Finally, there was another knock on the door. "Come in," called the little old lady, and in came a jolly face. "I can talk to you," she said. "You're the Muffin Man."

► End the story by singing "Do You Know the Muffin Man?"

Adaptations

► The rest of the children stand up or sit down to do the following motions. Demonstrate the actions below, and tell everyone they must repeat them whenever they are said in the story.

When the old lady rocks, rock back and forth.
When she spins, roll your hands around.
When she hears a knock at the door, pretend to knock on the door and make a clicking sound with your tongue.
When the old lady says, "Come in," wave with your hand.

► Change the Muffin Man to be Santa (boots, beard, red suit, mittens, coat, hat, etc.), the Easter Bunny (ears, feet, tail, paws, whiskers, etc.) or other characters.

The Treasure Box

When?

Here's a special story to tell using a sheet of paper to surprise children at the end of the day.

Why?

This story and the resulting treasure box will fascinate children.

What?

8 1/2" x 11" piece of paper

How?

▶ Tell the story below, following the directions for folding the paper.

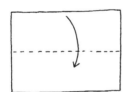

"The Treasure Box"

Once there were two children named Timmy and Tammy Tall.

And there were two children named Sam and Sheila Short.

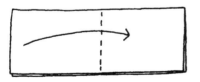

One day Timmy and Tammy received an invitation to a party and it looked like this. The invitation said, "Meet at the center."

So Timmy got all dressed up and went to the center. (Open the paper, then fold the right side into the middle.)

And Tammy got all dressed up and went to the center. (Fold the left side into the middle.)

When they got there they found a door, and they opened it and went inside. Now, Sam and Sheila got an invitation to the party, too, and it looked like this. The invitation said, "Meet at the center."

So Sam got all dressed up and went to the center. (Open the paper, then fold the right side into the middle.)

And Sheila got all dressed up and went to the center. (Fold in the left side.)

But when they got there the doors were locked, and they couldn't get inside.

They banged on the door and bent down the corner like this, but no one heard them. (Bend down top right corner.)

So they banged even louder and bent down the other side of the door, but still no one heard them. (Bend down top left corner.)

They kicked on the bottom of the the door and bent it in, too, but no one heard them. (Bend bottom corners.)

Finally, they realized that there was a little crack in the door that they could bend back a little like this on one side. (Fold back sides.)

And a little like this on the other side, and they could just squeeze inside the door.

And what do you think they found when they went inside? (Pull up the sides of the box and bend the ends up to form the treasure box.) They found a treasure box full of all kinds of treasures, just like the good times that we've had today.

Adaptations

▶ Let the children tell you what they've learned or enjoyed at school.

▶ Do this every day, selecting a different child to take the treasure box home.

A Story Box

When?

Pull out this little box between activities to occupy children while they are waiting.

Why?

Children enjoy repeating the gingerbread boy's chant as the story is told.

What?

school box or cigar box
felt scraps
fabric glue or glue gun
scissors
wiggly eyes

Preparation

▶ Cover the inside lid of the school box with felt to make a flannel board.

▶ Cut out the gingerbread boy and the other characters from felt using the illustrated patterns.

▶ Glue on the eyes, mouths and other details.

▶ Store the pieces in the box.

How?

▶ Tell the children that they can help you make some gingerbread cookies.

▶ First they will need to get out a big bowl. (Pretend to hold a bowl.)

▶ Next, let the children suggest different ingredients to put in the cookies. (Pretend to put these in and mix up the dough.)

▶ Have the children pretend to roll out the dough and cut out a gingerbread boy.

▶ Open the story box, and tell the traditional story of the gingerbread boy using the props in the story box.

▶ Encourage the children to say the following lines of the story with you.

*"Run, run, fast as you can.
You can't catch me, 'cause I'm the gingerbread man!"*

Adaptations

▶ Let the children act out the story.

▶ Make gingerbread cookies for snack.

▶ Make other flannel board story boxes.

LANGUAGE

Coffee Can Theater

When?

If there are a few extra minutes at story time, while waiting for all the children to come for a group activity or for entertaining a small group of children, pull out the coffee can theater and put on a performance.

Why?

Children develop their imaginations with this prop.

What?

large coffee can or other can with a lid
spray paint, wallpaper scraps, fabric, etc.
small toys, puppets and props

Preparation

▶ Decorate the outside of the can with spray paint, wallpaper scraps, fabric, etc.

▶ Place the toys in the can. (Use little figures, small dolls, stuffed animals, vehicles, trinkets, natural items, etc.)

How?

▶ When the children are sitting down, tell them there are special friends in the Coffee Can Theater that are going to tell a story.

▶ Pull out the characters and make up a story with the toys in the can.

Adaptations

▶ Let the children make up the story as you pull out the characters and props.

▶ Pass the can around the room, and let each child pull something out and add to the story.

▶▶▶▶▶▶ LANGUAGE ▶▶▶▶▶▶

Storyteller's Chair

When?

If half the class has finished cleaning up, washing their hands or has completed another activity, let them entertain each other by telling stories.

Why?

Storytelling is an old tradition that should be fostered in children. In addition to building oral language, it helps children develop confidence and good listening skills.

What?

director's chair, stool or other wooden chair
gold or silver spray paint
ribbons, glitter or other trimmings

Preparation

▶ Spray the chair with gold or silver spray paint.

▶ Write "Storyteller's Chair" on it and decorate with glitter, ribbons, etc.

How?

▶ Choose one child to sit in the chair and tell stories to the other children.

▶ Stories may be original or their versions of familiar folk tales and books.

Adaptations

▶ Let children read (or pretend to read) books to friends as they sit in the chair.

▶ Use a storyteller's hat, cape, magic wand or other props to encourage storytelling.

▶▶▶▶▶▶▶   LANGUAGE   ▶▶▶▶▶▶▶

Spider Web Story

When?

Use this story technique to begin circle time, reinforce a concept or book or to entertain children if there are a few extra minutes.

Why?

This group story enhances oral language, imagination, cooperation and other skills.

What?

ball of yarn

How?

▶ Have the children sit in a circle.

▶ Begin a story (tell a familiar story or make up a story).

▶ Wrap the yarn around your hand one time, then roll the ball of yarn to another child. (Demonstrate how to wrap the yarn loosely around the hand.)

▶ That child adds to the story, then rolls the ball to a friend.

▶ The story continues with each child adding to the story until you have created a yarn web in the middle of the circle.

▶ Since children often want to go on and on with this story, the teacher may want to bring closure to the tale at the end.

Adaptations

▶ Retell the story backwards, rolling up the ball of yarn.

▶ Make up a new ending to a familiar story, make up a story using the names of children in the class or tie the story in with a theme, season or holiday.

▶ Use the ball of yarn to tell an "I like my friend because..." story. One by one the children tell why they like another child in the class, then they pass the yarn to that friend who adds to the story by saying "I like my friend (another child's name) because..." Monitor carefully to be sure all the children are included at some point.

▶ Cut out magazine pictures and glue them to construction paper then let the children select one, and start a story about it.

▶ Tape record stories as the children tell them, then play them back so they can listen to themselves.

▶▶▶▶▶▶ LANGUAGE ▶▶▶▶▶▶

The Big Bag Book

When?

Use the bag book and other big books to promote reading readiness skills.

Why?

Logos children recognize provide successful reading opportunities for all children. They will also enjoy participating in collecting bags for this book.

What?

5-10 large paper grocery sacks
bags or sacks from stores and restaurants
scissors
glue
yarn

Preparation

▶ Cut the front and back off each grocery sack to make the pages for the book.

▶ Punch holes in the pages on one side and tie together with yarn. On the front cover write "Our Bag Book."

▶ Cut the store logo from the front of each of the other bags and glue it to a page in the book.

How?

▶ Ask the children to start collecting bags for a special book when they go shopping or get carry-out food.

▶ When you have several bags, put them together using the directions above.

▶ Let the children "read" the logos on the bags together, or choose one child to "read" it to the class

Adaptations

▶ Ask the children to dictate a sentence for each page, or use a repetitious sentence on each page.

▶ Let the children make their own bag books, or suggest to parents that they collect bags and make one with their child at home.

▶ Have childen cut off the front of cereal boxes. Punch holes in the sides and put them together with book rings. "Read" what everyone eats for breakfast.

Book Buddies

When?

Use Book Buddies before nap time or as children complete activities.

Why?

Sharing a book with a friend always makes it more fun.

What?

stuffed animals
big books, little books, books from the library, books children bring from home, homemade books
bookshelf

How?

▶ Make an attractive display with the books and animals.

▶ When the children are through with an activity or want something quiet to do, invite them to get a book and stuffed animal and "read" the book to their animal friend.

▶ Encourage the children to tell you about the book.

Adaptation

▶ Let the children look at books with friends at other in-between times during the day.

Mystery Person

When?

Use this language experience activity at circle time or at the end of the day.

Why?

The connection between written and spoken language is reinforced by this activity, as is children's self-esteem.

What?

large chart paper
markers

How?

▶ When the children are sitting down, take the marker and write "Mystery Person" at the top of the chart.

▶ Write and draw clues about a special person in the class.

▶ The children have to play detective to discover who the Mystery Person is.

▶ Ask the children to look at you.

▶ Write the following clue.

My eyes are (color).

▶ Use pictures and the appropriate color markers to illustrate the clues. For example, use blue to draw blue eyes, brown to draw brown hair, etc.

▶ Ask the children to "read" the clue.

▶ Point to each word.

▶ Next, write the second clue.

My hair is (color).

▶ Again, read the clue together.

▶ Continue writing and reading clues about the Mystery Person's favorite food, songs, stories, games, pets, family, etc.

▶ Tell the children when they think they know who it is to smile.

▶ At the bottom of the chart write "Who am I?"

▶ Read over the entire chart, asking the Mystery Person to stand up at the end. (Make the clues fairly obvious and look directly at that person.)

▶ The Mystery Person can draw her picture at the bottom of the page and take it home.

Adaptation

▶ Use a class attendance list and mark off each child when she is the Mystery Person so you don't leave anyone out.

Story Headbands

When?

Story dramatizations are a fun way to extend story time or entertain children.

Why?

Spark language skills and imaginations with simple costumes and props.

What?

sentence strips or poster board cut into 3" x 22" strips
scissors
glue
markers
paper clips
construction paper

Preparation

▶ Draw the heads of various story characters on construction paper.

▶ Color them, cut them out, and glue them to the sentence strips or poster board to make headbands.

▶ Fit them to the child's head and secure with paper clips.

How?

▶ After reading or telling a story to the children, discuss the main characters, the setting and the different events.

▶ Let the children choose which characters they would like to be, put on the headbands and act out the story. (For younger children, the teacher will need to be the narrator and give guidance as the story is performed.)

▶ If time permits, choose other children and let them act out the story.

Adaptations

▶ Let children make their own story headbands for acting out stories, rhymes or songs.

▶ Let children make up new endings to old, familiar stories.

▶ Glue felt ears, horns and other details to plastic headbands to make story props.

▶ Place story props and costumes in the housekeeping area for children to play with.

 LANGUAGE ▶▶▶▶▶▶

Flannel Board

When?

Focus children's attention with a flannel board activity to engage them at in-between times or when they have to wait.

Why?

The visuals on the flannel board will give meaning to stories, songs and other concepts.

What?

fabric bolt board (free at fabric stores)
felt (1/2 yard)
felt scraps
scissors
glue gun or fabric glue

Preparation

▶ Cut the felt so it fits around the fabric bolt board.

▶ Glue in place.

▶ From felt scraps, cut out different characters, animals or shapes. The flannel board can be used for storytelling, for music visuals, for math, etc.

How?

▶ Place the felt pieces on the flannel board and demonstrate how to tell stories, group objects, make patterns, etc.

▶ Let the children freely play with the different felt characters and make up stories.

Adaptations

▶ Cover a portion of a bulletin board, the front of a desk or the back of a shelf with felt to be used for flannel board stories and songs.

▶ In addition to felt, pellon can be colored to make objects for the flannel board.

▶ If felt pieces don't stick well, attach a little piece of velcro (hook side out) to the back.

▶▶▶▶▶▶ LANGUAGE ▶▶▶▶▶▶

Magazine Rack

When?

Let children look at magazines as they wait for others to complete an activity, before or after naps, etc.

Why?

Exposing children to a variety of printed materials encourages lifelong reading skills.

What?

magazines (children's magazines, nature and sports magazines or any child-oriented publications)
travel brochures
menus
catalogs
maps
magazine rack, basket or other container

How?

▶ As the children complete projects or centers, encourage them to select a magazine, sit down and look at it.

▶ Magazines can also help children relax before rest, or children who wake early can entertain themselves quietly by looking at them.

Adaptations

▶ Ask parents to donate old magazines.

▶ Cut out appropriate cartoons from the funny pages, glue them to construction paper and make "comic books" for the children.

LANGUAGE

Big Joke Book

When?

Use the Big Joke Book to extend story time or to entertain children any time throughout the day.

Why?

Children will have fun making this book and will appreciate their own sense of humor.

What?

poster board (cut in half)
crayons or markers
hole punch
book rings (pipe cleaners cut in half can also be used)

How?

➤ Divide children up into pairs and give each pair half a sheet of poster board.

➤ Have the children dictate a riddle or joke on the front of the poster.

➤ Then have them illustrate the joke or riddle, drawing the answer on the back.

➤ Punch holes in the posters when they are finished and attach the pages together with book rings.

➤ Make a cover page titled "Our Big Joke Book."

➤ Let the children take turns guessing the jokes and riddles.

Adaptations

➤ Older children could write their own jokes and riddles.

➤ Allow the children to take the Big Joke Book home and share it with their families.

▶▶▶▶▶▶▶   LANGUAGE   ▶▶▶▶▶▶▶

Imagination Bag

When?

Use the imagination bag to capture children's interest.

Why?

This activity encourages children to use their imagination and contributes to language and concept development.

What?

paper lunch sacks

How?

▶ Have children sit down on the floor, then give each a paper sack.

▶ Tell the children it's their imagination bag and that they are going to build a farm with the things in the bag.

▶ Have the children open their bags.

▶ Ask who sees something they can put on their farm.

▶ As the children name different animals, people, equipment and other items found on the farm, have them pretend to take them out and put them on the floor as they build their farm.

▶ When time is up, or before children become bored, ask them to pick up the animals, the fence, farmer, etc. and put them back in their bags.

▶ Collect the bags and save them for another day.

Adaptations

▶ Vary the "contents" of the Imagination Bags. Take a trip to the moon, prehistoric times, the enchanted woods, the bottom of the ocean or any other time and place of interest.

▶ How about a pretend pet show? Give each child a two foot piece of string or yarn. Let them walk around one at a time and describe the imaginary pet on the end of the string.

Journals

When?

Journals provide a quiet, independent activity for children as they arrive at school in the morning, after nap or at the end of the day.

Why?

Children have the opportunity to write, scribble or draw and to express their thoughts and ideas in a risk-free way.

What?

spiral ring notebook
pencil
crayons

How?

▶ Ask each child to bring in a spiral ring notebook.

▶ When they come in the morning, let them get their journals and begin to draw or write.

▶ Be available to take their dictation.

▶ Set aside a special time for the children to share what is in their journals.

Adaptations

▶ Save journals throughout the school year as part of the child's assessment portfolio. They tell a story about the child.

▶ Use journals at the end of the day for children to recall what they have done at school.

▶ Make a different journal for each month. Give the children a piece of construction paper to decorate for the cover. Count out the number of pages they will need and staple them in the book.

▶ Make a "Good Book" for each child and let them draw pictures and write stories about good things they do or what they like about themselves.

▶▶▶▶▶▶ 12 ▶▶▶▶▶▶

CLOSURE

Just as you start the day with positive thoughts, it's important to end the day with good feelings. Bring the children back together, sing some songs and review all the things you've done. This closing time is a meaningful ritual for you and the children, and a special way to say good-bye.

At the closing circle time, it is helpful to recall favorite activities and go over the day in sequential order. (That way activities will be fresh in children's minds when parents ask, "What did you do today?") Also, tell the children something special about tomorrow so they'll anticipate coming back.

Take a few minutes at the end of the busy day to reflect, think positive thoughts and say, "It's been a good day!"

So comes the closure to this book. Enjoy it, adapt it and use it to fill the day with happy memories. And remember, the love you give will always come back.

Love grows
One by one,
Two by two,
And four by four.
Love grows
Round and round
And comes right back
To your door.

 CLOSING SONG

The More We Get Together

When?

Tie up the many pieces from the day with this closing song.

Why?

Social relationships and group feelings are enhanced as children sing.

What?

No materials are needed.

How?

➤ Sit or stand in a circle.

➤ Hold on to each other's shoulders.

➤ Sway and sing.

> *The more we get together,*
> *Together, together,*
> *The more we get together,*
> *The happier we'll be.*
> *For your friends are my friends,*
> *And my friends are your friends.*
> *The more we get together,*
> *The happier we'll be.*

Adaptations

➤ Insert children's names in the song.

> *There's (child's name) and (name),*
> *And (name), and (name).*
> *These are all my friends*
> *As you can see.*

➤ Here's another song to end the day on a positive note. Sing it to the tune of "Goodnight Ladies."

> *We had a good day.*
> *We had a good day.*
> *We had a good day.*
> *We had a good day at school.*
> *See you tomorrow. (wave good-bye)*
> *See you tomorrow.*
> *See you tomorrow.*
> *See you tomorrow at school.*

▶▶▶▶▶▶ REVIEWING THE DAY ▶▶▶▶▶▶

Daily News

When?

After a busy day, review all the activities with the Daily News.

Why?

In addition to contributing to reading skills, the Daily News helps children recall what they've learned.

What?

chart paper
marker

How?

▶ Have the children sit down.

▶ Write Daily News and the day's date at the top of the chart paper.

▶ Ask, "Who can remember the first thing we did this morning?"

▶ Choose a child, then write down what she dictates to you on the chart paper.

▶ Continue writing what other children recall.

▶ If needed, prompt them by asking what they made at art, what their story was about, what they cooked for snack, etc.

▶ Hang the Daily News on the door so parents can read about all the activities when they pick up their children.

Adaptations

▶ Choose different children to draw illustrations on the language experience chart.

▶ Rewrite the Daily News on a regular sheet of paper, then photocopy one for each child to take home.

▶ Let children draw pictures of what they learned or liked best at school at the end of the day.

Happy Thoughts

When?

Gather children together and fill them with Happy Thoughts before they leave.

Why?

This activity fosters positive feelings about school and friends.

What?

No materials are needed.

How?

➤ Ask the children to sit in a circle.

➤ Then go around and whisper a word of encouragement in each child's ear.

➤ Tell them to look at the friends sitting next to them and say something nice to each friend.

Adaptation

➤ Play this hugging game.

Simon says touch your knees.
Simon says touch your head.
Simon says give yourself a big hand. (clap, clap)
Simon says give yourself a big hug for having such a good day at school. (mmmm!)

 INVOLVING PARENTS

Activity Calendars

September

Sunday	Monday	Tuesday	Wednesday	Thursday	Friday	Saturday
	1 Eat an apple.	2 Play catch.	3 Sing Twinkle Twinkle.	4 Nighttime Walk	5 Make a puppet.	6 Work a puzzle.
7 Be kind to an animal.	8 Run, jump, hop.	9 Read a book.	10 Count your chairs.	11 Cook dinner.	12 Say a nursery rhyme.	13 Draw chalk pictures.
14 Give someone a hug. XXOO	15 Draw your family.	16 Make a cookie cutter sandwich.	17 Make up a dance.	18 Make a necklace	19 Make a poster together.	20 Clean your room.
21 Go outside.	22 Make a salad.	23 Sing pretty songs.	24 Do a leaf rubbing.	25 Make homemade dough.	26 Go on a shape hunt.	27 Play a game together.
28 Say please and thank-you.	29 Make something with boxes.	30 Tell a story.				

When?

Give each child an activity calendar at the beginning of every month.

Why?

Children will look forward to spending some quality time with their parents each day doing the activities.

What?

blank calendar

Preparation

▶ Decorate the calendar.

▶ Write down an activity, song or special project children can do each day with their parents. Reinforce concepts the children are learning or relate an activity to books and themes. (See illustration.)

How?

▶ Make parents an integral part of the school program by letting them know that they are their child's first and most important teacher.

▶ Indeed, the more involved parents are, the more successful their children will be.

▶ Write a letter to parents explaining that the children will bring home a calendar at the beginning of each month so the parents can reinforce some of the skills the children are learning at school.

▶ Suggest that they put the calendar on their refrigerator and set aside a special time each evening to do the activities together.

Adaptation

▶ Make a special calendar for the children to use over summer vacation.

 INVOLVING PARENTS

Super Sacks

When?

Pass out Super Sacks to children just before they go home.

Why?

Super Sacks reinforce skills children are learning at school, involve parents in the program and help children develop responsibility.

What?

lunch sacks (one for each child)
markers or crayons

Preparation

Depending on what the children are learning, write or draw one of the following on each sack:

> **shapes** *(Draw a circle, square, triangle, etc.)*
> **colors** *(Scribble a color or write the color word.)*
> **numerals** *(Write numerals. Ask children to bring in that number of objects the next day.)*
> **senses** *(Draw an eye, hand, ear, etc. Ask children to bring in something they like to see, touch, hear, etc.)*

> **letters** *(Print letters on the bags. Ask children to find something that starts with that sound.)*
> **me** *(Ask the child to find something special about himself.)*
> **family** *(Bring in a family photo or keepsake.)*
> **animal, person, plant** *or other objects related to what the children are learning*

How?

- ► Tell the children that you have something for them to do with their parents.

- ► Give each child a bag and go over what he should do with it.

- ► Give the children examples, then let them repeat the directions to you.

- ► When children return with their sacks the following day, share them at circle time, or set up a special shelf or table in the room where children can display objects.

Adaptations

- ► Older children can draw or write on their own super sacks.

- ► Have a few extra items on hand to help out children who forget.

 INVOLVING PARENTS

Take Home Kits

When?

Encourage children and parents to check these out and take them home at the end of the day.

Why?

Besides building a home/school partnership, the activities in these kits suggest other materials parents can give their children to play with at home.

What?

detergent boxes with handles
spray paint

Preparation

▶ Spray paint the boxes, or let the children decorate them.

▶ Fill the boxes with the following kits or materials:

writer's kit—blank paper, envelopes, pens, pencils, tape, etc.
math kit—ruler, dice, set cards, shape stencils, paper and pencils, play money, etc.
art kit—scissors, markers, crayons, paper, glue, paper sacks, paper plates, collage materials, etc.
science kit—magnifying glass, magnet, collections of shells, rocks, seeds, etc.

blank books and markers
sewing cards
play dough and cookie cutters
cut up straws, pasta with holes and yarn to string them on
puppets or little toys, books, children's magazines
scrap paper and hole punch
homemade puzzles (Cut up the front of cardboard food boxes into puzzle shapes.)
homemade card games and matching games

How?

▶ Put the directions in the box.

▶ Let the children choose a different one to take home every night or week.

 INVOLVING PARENTS

Buddy Bunny

When?

Buddy Bunny chooses a different child to go home with every day.

Why?

Language skills and parental involvement are enhanced with this take-home story.

What?

stuffed animal (bunny, bear, etc.)
cloth bag or backpack
spiral ring notebook

Preparation

▶ Put the bunny (or other animal) in the backpack or bag, along with the notebook.

▶ Write a note to go in the bag similar to the following one.

Dear Parents,
Today your child is bringing home Buddy Bunny. Buddy loves children and he loves to get into mischief. Please write a story in the notebook about what Buddy does with your child. You may want to let your child dictate a story for you to write. We'll read the story tomorrow at school.
Thank you! Have fun!

How?

▶ Choose a different child each day to take Buddy Bunny and the bag home.

▶ Read what the parents have written the next morning at circle time.

Adaptations

▶ Add a book, toothbrush, change of clothes or other props to go along with Buddy Bunny.

▶ Older children can write their own adventures with Buddy Bunny.

 INVOLVING PARENTS

Note Tote

When?

Fill the Note Tote with children's paintings, letters to parents and other papers at the end of the day.

Why?

Sometimes children drop their papers. This will be a handy way to keep things together.

What?

cardboard rollers (paper towel rolls)
markers
crayons
stickers
collage materials

Preparation

▶ Give each child a cardboard roller. Write her name on it.

▶ Let the children decorate their rollers with markers, crayons, stickers, magazine pictures or other collage materials.

How?

▶ Before the children go home, tell them to get their papers, roll them up and put them in their Note Tote.

▶ Have them pretend they are mail carriers and deliver their notes and pictures to their parents.

Adaptations

▶ Give children large grocery sacks to decorate to take their work home in.

▶ Let children decorate detergent boxes with handles to use to take home papers.

NOTES

INDEX

500 Five Minute Games
Quick and Easy Activities for 3-6 Year Olds

Jackie Silberg

Enjoy five-minute fun with the newest book from the author who brought you the popular series **Games to Play with Babies**, **Games to Play With Toddlers**, and **Games to Play With Two Year Olds**. These games are easy, fun, developmentally appropriate, and promote learning in just five spare minutes of the day. Children unwind, get the giggles out, communicate, and build self-esteem as they have fun. Each game indicates the particular skill developed. 270 pages.

ISBN 0-87659-172-1   **Gryphon House**
16455   **Paperback**

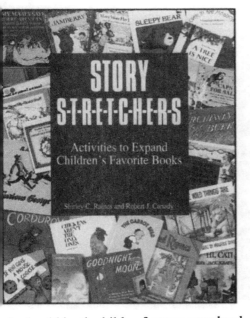

"..should be the bible of every preschool and early primary teacher in America".

–Jim Trelease, author,
The New Read-Aloud Handbook

Story S-t-r-e-t-c-h-e-r-s®:
Activities to Expand Children's Favorite Books (Pre-K and K)

Shirley C. Raines and Robert J. Canady

Here is a perfect way to connect children's enthusiasm for books with other areas of the curriculum. Using 450 ideas from children's best-loved picture books, children will experience exciting activities provided for a variety of learning centers in science, nature, math, movement and more. 256 pages.

ISBN 0-87659-119-5   **Gryphon House**
10011   **Paperback**

Preschool Art
It's the Process, Not the Product

MaryAnn Kohl

Anyone working with preschoolers and early primary age children will want this book. Over 200 activities teach children to explore and understand their world through open-ended art experiences that emphasize the process of art, not the product. The first chapter introduces basic art activities appropriate for all children, while subsequent chapters, which build on the activities in the first chapter, are divided by seasons. With activities that include painting, drawing, collage, sculpture and construction, this is the only art book you will need. 260 pages.

ISBN 0-87659-168-3   **Gryphon House**
16985   **Paperback**

Where is Thumbkin?
500 Activities to Use with Songs You Already Know

Pam Schiller, Thomas Moore

These are the songs teachers and children are already singing together every day. The book is organized month-by-month, and has sections for toddlers, threes, fours, five and six year olds. These simple learning activities can be used in circle time, for transitions, or for special music time. A list of related children's literature and recordings accompanies each set of activities. 256 pages.

ISBN 0-87659-164-0   **Gryphon House**
13156   **Paperback**

The GIANT Encyclopedia of Theme Activities For Children 2 to 5

Over 600 Favorite Activities
Created by Teachers for Teachers

The result of a nationwide contest, this book offers 48 themes and clear descriptions of 600 ready-to-use teacher-developed activities. From the alphabet and art to winter and zoo, you will find themes for every season and every day of the year.

All activities require minimum preparation and have been proven successful in the classroom. This book has a special strengthened binding, allowing it to lie flat on a table. An ideal resource for a busy teacher. 512 pages.

ISBN 0-87659-166-7   **Gryphon House**
19216   **Paperback**

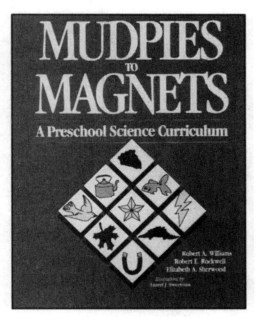

Mudpies to Magnets

A Preschool Science Curriculum

Elizabeth A. Sherwood, Robert A. Williams,
Robert E. Rockwell

224 hands-on science experiments and ideas with step-by-step instructions delight and amaze children as they experience nature, the human body, electricity, floating and sinking and more. Children participate in ready-made projects such as making a tornado in a jar, creating constellations and growing crystals. Categorized by curriculum areas, each activity includes a list of vocabulary words. 157 pages.

ISBN 0-87659-112-8   **Gryphon House**
10005   **Paperback**